If . . . Then . . . Curriculum: Assessment-Based Instruction, Kindergarten

Lucy Calkins with Colleagues from the Teachers College Reading and Writing Project

Photography by Peter Cunningham

HEINEMANN ◆ PORTSMOUTH, NH

Heinemann
361 Hanover Street
Portsmouth, NH 03801–3912
www.heinemann.com

Offices and agents throughout the world

© 2013 by Lucy Calkins

Cataloging-in-Publication data is on file with the Library of Congress.

ISBN-13: 978-0-325-04810-9
Production: Elizabeth Valway, David Stirling and Abigail Heim
Cover and interior designs: Jenny Jensen Greenleaf
Series includes photographs by Peter Cunningham, Nadine Baldasare, and Elizabeth Dunford
Composition: Publishers' Design and Production Services, Inc.
Manufacturing: Steve Bernier

Printed in the United States of America on acid-free paper
21 20 19 18 17 VP 2 3 4 5 6

Contents

PART TWO: Differentiating Instruction for Individuals and Small Groups: If . . . Then . . . Conferring Scenarios

Introduction

Kindergarten Writers and Planning Your Year

There is perhaps no year more crucial than kindergarten. What students learn this first year provides the building blocks not just for each subsequent year's instruction and learning, but more importantly, for children's experience of the written word and their identities as people who write. Your kindergartners will come to you full of stories and information. Some will come from homes in which parents invite their sons and daughters to add to the shopping list or to write stories for dolls and teddy bears, and some will come from pre-K classrooms in which children are invited to write, tell, and act stories. But in many cases, it will be you who will introduce kids to the world of written language. This is an enormously important responsibility. You will be the one to teach the children in your classroom that they belong to the world of written language. You will convey that little marks on the page tell stories, carry jokes, give orders, change the world. And you will guide each child in your care to believe that those little marks on the page will be a source of joy and laughter, friendship, and power.

AN OVERVIEW OF THE EXPECTATIONS AND SUPPORTS IN THE KINDERGARTEN UNITS

The data show that at least two-thirds of children enter kindergarten already knowing their letters and sounds. Those children are ready to write whole sentences underneath their pictures, starting the first week of kindergarten. Because we would rather err on the side of being too supportive rather than not supportive enough, the units we outline for kindergartners in this series have been written with a more diverse kindergarten in mind. We've planned these books assuming that many of your children enter kindergarten knowing only some of their letters and sounds. You may also have students who know several letters and sounds but do not know how to put them together to write words and sentences.

If your students are notably more proficient than this, you may want to skip some of the more foundational units and rely on the more advanced units in this book. Possible pathways are outlined in the following section, "If… Then: Assessment-Based Planning."

No matter what your children's knowledge of letters and sounds may be, chances are that they can recall something they have done, put that event onto the page however they can (for most this will mean by making pictures), and tell the story of the event. It's also likely that kindergartners will have no trouble thinking about a topic on which they are experts and then teaching others all about that topic. So you'll want to teach writing in ways that capitalize on your children's yearning to tell their stories, to teach the topics they know, and you'll want to *avoid* suggesting that writers need to learn and draw on tons of strategies to come up with an idea for writing.

Throughout the unit books, there are many opportunities for students to engage in close study of the grade level complex texts that function as mentor texts for a given unit of study. You will see we have paid enormous attention to ensuring that students are given opportunities to engage in work that places high levels of cognitive demand on them. They are continually asked to transfer what they learn while working in one text or one genre to another text in another genre. Students engage in inquiries and evaluate mentor texts, their own writing, and writing written by peers. They also set goals for themselves and receive assistance in working with resolve toward those goals.

All of this work sets your children up to succeed not only with the four main unit books, but also with the additional or alternative units you decide

to round out your year with. In the following section, I outline several different pathways for integrating the unit overviews offered in this book into your
curriculum, based on your students' needs, strengths, and interests.

IF... THEN: ASSESSMENT-BASED PLANNING

You will want to assess your students early on. Some children begin the year
with a knowledge of letters and sounds and of genres of writing. You may question whether this is, in fact, true of your students. In 2012, we began the school
year by asking hundreds of kindergartners to do a piece of on-demand opinion
writing and on-demand information writing, as well as the on-demand narrative, and we were flabbergasted by how much children already know, even at
the start of kindergarten. You can decide whether to start by assessing all three
genres or to instead assess just one (many teachers begin by assessing narrative writing) and to hold off until later on in the year to administer the others.

Many teachers use the narrative assessment found in the assessment book
of this series, *Writing Pathways: Performance Assessments and Learning Progressions*, to evaluate their kindergartners at the start of the year (and again
at additional points throughout the year to track students' progress). If you
begin with the first book in this series, *Launching the Writing Workshop*, then
you will probably want to begin with the narrative assessment. In *Launching*,
children will first be asked to write about things they know well and, later in
that unit, they will write stories. You might also, or instead, assess your children
with the information writing assessment. A third option is to use both assessments. No matter which on-demand assessment you use early on to assess your
youngsters, chances are that many children will produce drawings, not words,
which may or may not be representational. This is data that will inform your
teaching, especially at the start of the year. You will certainly want to record
what children say they have "written" on the page so that you will have an idea
of your children's sense of story or of information writing. Just because they
don't yet have the tools to record their ideas doesn't mean that your youngsters
lack things to say.

If, after teaching *Launching the Writing Workshop*, you feel that your
students could use some additional practice with labeling and writing simple
sentences, then you may opt to teach either the "Storytelling across the Pages:
First Steps for Personal Narrative Writing" or the "Looking Closely" unit, both
described in this book. Both units are full of nuts-and-bolts instruction that
will help your youngsters get more writing onto the page.

If you are finding that your children write in such a fashion that each page is
a fresh new idea, with little or no connection between pages, then "Storytelling
across the Pages" will be an especially well-chosen unit for your students. It is
also a good unit for your class if your students spent lots and lots of time drawing
during the first month but seems to be ill at ease saying stories to accompany
those drawings. This unit will highlight storytelling. Then, too, if many of your
students who are obsessed with copying letters or words from around the room
but attach little or no meaning to the print, this will be a good choice. This unit
emphasizes that, first and foremost, the job of a narrative writer is to tell a story.

If, after you teach the *Launching* unit, many of your students need additional practice learning their letters or sounds and getting words onto the
page, you may want to teach the alternate unit, "Looking Closely: Observing,
Labeling, and Listing Like Scientists," before teaching the *Writing for Readers* unit. "Looking Closely" is chock full of practical tips for learners who are
at the beginning stages of writing; that is, ones who are still working to put
words onto paper. Built into this unit are lessons for helping students create
labeled, detailed pictures and lessons, too, on writing sentences. This unit
teaches fundamental literary skills while children act like scientists, so it will
be especially popular with children who want to collect, sort, categorize and
study leaves and other bits of the natural world. If, however, your children had
great success during the *Launching* unit and are ready to move past labeling to
writing sentences, you may instead progress to the second book in this series.

The "Writing All-About Books" unit is intended as a foundational all-about
information unit. During this unit, kids write lots and lots of simple information books. This unit would probably come after you teach the *How-To Books*
unit. The unit allows children to write expository information texts on any
topic they want.

You may decide to teach "Writing Pattern Books to Read, Write, and Teach"
to emphasize reading-writing connections, since your students will surely be
reading and studying pattern books as readers of them. The final two units in
this book, "Music in Our Hearts: Writing Songs and Poetry" and "With a Little
Help from My Friends: Independent Writing Projects across the Genres," are
especially rich units for your students. "Music in Our Hearts" teaches children
to be more conscious of the crafting decisions they make and also teaches
close reading. "With a Little Help from My Friends" is a cross-genre unit that
works especially well at the end of the year, since it fosters students' growing
independence and draws on their knowledge of many types of writing. This
unit allows students to reflect on their growth as writers across the year.

Storytelling across the Pages
First Steps for Personal Narrative Writing

RATIONALE/INTRODUCTION

This unit will invite kindergartners to embark on work that will surely dazzle you and the kids. Expect the unit to be a smash hit! In this unit you will explicitly teach students to tell organized, structured stories that proceed chronologically through the sequence of a small event. If you have the video *Big Lessons from Small Writers* (and we urge you to get it if you do not), you'll want to watch the young writers work on their true stories—especially Harold, who writes, "I woke up. I put on my pants, I put on my shoes. Then I walked to school." That's the work of this unit.

This unit is a sort of precursor to the work children will do in the *Writing for Readers* unit. In that book, Lucy Calkins and Natalie Louis show you how children can begin to write stories that others can read, writing meaningful moments from their very own lives and using all that they know about spelling and conventions to make their writing easy for others to read. All of this work is in line with most state standards, which channel kindergartners to produce narrative stories through a combination of drawing and writing and add to do this in such a way that they narrate a single event or several loosely linked events. You might also look to the Rubric for Narrative Writing, available in the online resources, to set goals for their narrative writing across the year.

Some goals of the unit, then, are for your youngsters to generate true stories from their lives, recording these stories across the pages of little booklets using representational drawings. You'll want them to tell cohesive, sequenced narratives, and label many items on each page. You'll want children to be able to "reread" the books they write, turning the pages from front to back, "reading" them from left to right, top to bottom. They will work in partnerships, sharing their booklets. You'll want them to tell their stories using rich, oral storytelling language. They can sit hip-to-hip, hold the booklet between them, turn pages (ideally from left to right), and tell the story as they study the pictures and "read" the writing. They can begin working on one-to-one matches as they name the things that they see on the page and read the labels under each of those items.

Another goal in this unit is to help children learn to hear and record the sounds in words, stretching each word out so they can isolate and hear the sounds at the start of the word, making a mark to represent that sound. You'll teach children that they can listen to the sound, think, "What letter makes that sound?" and try out different letters, relying on what they know about letter names and sounds to make a match. They can then reread what they have written—the initial sound—and try to hear another sound, continuing in that fashion. Your expectation will be that many of the children will write using initial and final consonant sounds, relying on letter names when they do not know the sounds a letter makes. According to most state standards, by the end of kindergarten, your writers should be writing letters for most consonant and short-vowel sounds, so it is important to teach them to isolate phonemes, even if they do not yet know how to write the corresponding letter. By the end of the month, if not before, some of your children will have graduated from writing random letters and initial consonants only, to hearing and recording more of the sounds in their words, perhaps even writing phrases or simple sentences to go along with their pictures.

A SUMMARY OF THE BENDS IN THE ROAD FOR THIS UNIT

In Bend I (Writers Write: Become a Storyteller and Then Get That Story Down!), you'll invite your children to become storytellers. You'll suggest that real-life storytellers—family members, famous storytellers, can be mentors. You'll teach children how to draw their stories so that they will remember exactly who was there and what the person was doing, and you'll help them to record events in sequence, across the pages of a booklet. Plan to spend almost two weeks in this bend.

In Bend II (Writers Use What They Know about Letters and Sounds to Spell Words When They Write), the focus will turn toward getting more letters and sounds, labels, and sentences down onto the page. You'll spend a week teaching children a number of strategies for hearing and recording sounds in words, making their writing easier to read.

Rubric for Narrative Writing–Kindergarten

	Pre-Kindergarten (2 POINTS)	2.5 PTS	Kindergarten (3 POINTS)	3.5 PTS	Grade 1 (4 POINTS)	SCORE
STRUCTURE						
Overall	The writer told a story with pictures and some "writing."	Mid-level	The writer told, drew, and wrote a whole story.	Mid-level	The writer wrote about when she did something.	
Lead	The writer started by drawing or saying something.	Mid-level	The writer had a page that showed what happened first.	Mid-level	The writer tried to make a beginning for his story.	
Transitions	The writer kept on working.	Mid-level	The writer put his pages in order.	Mid-level	The writer put her pages in order. She used words such as and then, so.	
Ending	The writer's story ended.	Mid-level	The writer had a page that showed what happened last in her story.	Mid-level	The writer found a way to end his story.	
Organization	On the writer's paper, there was a place for drawing and a place where she tried to write words.	Mid-level	The writer's story had a page for the beginning, a page for the middle, and a page for the end.	Mid-level	The writer wrote her story across three or more pages.	
						TOTAL
DEVELOPMENT						
Elaboration*	The writer put more and then more on the page.	Mid-level	The writer's story indicated who was there, what they did, and how the characters felt.	Mid-level	The writer put the picture from his mind onto the page. He had details in pictures and words.	(X 2)
Craft*	In the writer's story, she told and showed what happened.	Mid-level	The writer drew and wrote some details about what happened.	Mid-level	The writer used labels and words to give details.	(X 2)
						TOTAL

* Elaboration and Craft are double-weighted categories: Whatever score a student would get in these categories is worth double the amount of points. For example, if a student exceeds expectations in Elaboration, then that student would receive 8 points instead of 4 points. If a student meets standards in Elaboration, then that student would receive 6 points instead of 3 points.

In Bend III (Writers Revise Their Writing, Growing Their Stories Longer and Longer), you'll teach children how to say even more. You'll begin this week emphasizing to students the importance of rehearsing their stories aloud over and over—and over and over—before drawing and writing the words; this will lead to longer, clearer, more expressive stories. Then you'll introduce strategies for revising the writing that students have been collecting in their writing folders.

In Bend IV (Revising, Editing, and Fancying Up One Special Story for Publishing), each child will select a special story to revise and edit. They'll spend one to two days preparing their pieces for a publishing party, and the unit will end with a special writing celebration.

GETTING READY
Choose Mentor Storytellers and Gather Texts for Students

To support the work of this unit, you may want to select a few real-live storytellers that you'll reference often. Perhaps you'll choose someone you know personally: a cousin who loves to tell tall tales or your grandfather. Or perhaps you'll choose a professional storyteller such as Lester Laminack, Heather Forest, or Carmen Agra Deedy. All of these author/storytellers are fine examples of writers who also story-tell aloud with expression and drama. You might collect audio or video clips of some of these storytellers to share with your children. You'll also want to plan to read aloud rich, engaging literature that exemplifies personal narratives and storytelling. Some examples include *A Day with Daddy* by Nikki Grimes, *The Snowy Day* by Ezra Jack Keats, *Caps for Sale* by Esphyr Slobodkina, and *Three Billy Goats Gruff* by Paul Galdone. You may also want to consider revising your daily schedule slightly, to include five or ten minutes somewhere in your day outside of writing workshop for storytelling time. Ideally this would take place at the very start of the day, or just after kids return to the classroom after lunch, while stories about their morning or lunch or recess are fresh on their minds, ready to be told aloud.

Choose When and How Children Will Publish

In this unit, each of your kindergartners will select one of the many stories he or she has written for publishing. They'll spend a day or two "fancying up" their pieces, adding a few features and editing their work a bit. Then, for the final celebration, you might invite each child to bring a stuffed animal to school and then "read" the story to the stuffed animal. These creatures can become a listening zoo and work as alternatives to partners. Alternatively, you might have a special parade around the classroom or the school to celebrate the work of the unit. The parade might end at the bulletin board, with each child tacking his or her piece into the appropriate square.

BEND I: WRITERS WRITE: BECOME A STORYTELLER AND THEN GET THAT STORY DOWN!

Invite students into the world of storytelling by exposing them to your favorite storytellers. Give students the opportunity to write and tell stories from their own lives.

If you are launching this unit, it is because you want to give your children more experience with the world of storytelling. It makes sense, then, to invite them not just to make books, but to *story-tell*. Just think of your favorite storytellers—maybe a family member or a teacher you know who tells great stories or your favorite professional author/storytellers. Perhaps you'll play one of Heather Forest's recordings, or you'll show a video of Carmen Agra Deedy. Maybe you'll invite your storytelling brother into the classroom to tell one of his fishing tales, or your mother will come in and tell a story about when you were just a little child. Of course, you could always tell your own story, embellishing it with drama, expression, gestures, and a little bravado.

Gather your little ones around you and lean in close. Point out all the books that surround your meeting area. Tell children that every one of those books have been written by an author, a storyteller, and that they, too, can be storytellers. You might say to them, "This very day, every one of you is a storyteller." Then, demonstrate that authors tell great stories about the things they have done or that have happened to them. To do this, they think of one thing they did or one thing that happened to them, to remember that one time, and pretend it is happening all over again. Then they say out loud everything that happened in that one experience, one thing at a time. Voilà! They are storytellers!

"Then, the very next step," you'll tell your students, "will be to take a booklet, and on that very first page, draw what you remember you did *first*." You might demonstrate by drawing, say, how you sat on a bench at a shoe store, trying on a pair of sneakers. Then, flip to the next page, and draw what happened next. Maybe this is a picture of you paying for the shoes at the counter. Then, on the next page, perhaps a picture of you, at home, putting on the shoes and jumping up and down with them on. Be sure to model telling a story to go along with each picture, in full sentences with rich storytelling language. For those of you who have learned about the value of Small Moment stories you are right to notice that we aren't prioritizing focus as much as we will in that later unit.

From the first day of this unit, you will want to provide children with booklets and invite them to draw and write the true stories of their lives. It's reasonable to expect that students will be able to story-tell aloud and then draw and write a story in just a day or more. If you started with *Launching the Writing Workshop*, this may differ from the way your children wrote at the beginning of that unit; you probably started by giving them single sheets of paper on which to write. Now you'll want to begin with prestapled booklets (including some with blank pages, some with a line or two on each page) and put these out in trays at your writing center.

The truth is that young kids can do a lot with independence. When most kids are working with blocks or crayons, they don't need to stop every three minutes to ask, "Now what?" or "Is this right?" They tend to work with engagement, confidence, and zeal. A kindergarten writing workshop should feel a lot like block time, with kids having and pursuing their own wonderful ideas. For this to happen, you need to be ready to accept children's approximations with pleasure. You need to imagine kids initiating, working on, and completing their "writing" as best they are able, moving from one story to another with verve and confidence, even though the work they produce at first will likely consist of drawings that are perhaps challenging to decipher, some letters, some known words, perhaps even some made-up squiggles and pretend-writing—for now.

Immerse students in rich stories and storytelling language by telling and retelling stories as well as reading aloud stories that resemble the personal narratives that your students will be writing.

Some children will come to school with a strong background in storytelling, while others may not have that experience. For children to write stories, they'll need to hear stories told to them and read to them. A deep immersion in the sound of storytelling language will help children as they now try to write the episodes of their lives as stories, and you'll want to remind them that what they are doing during writing time is writing stories, just like those they are reading during reading time. It will help if you read and reread and reread again some stories that resemble the personal narratives your children will be writing. Hopefully, outside the writing workshop, throughout the school day, you will find many opportunities to read and reread stories filled to the brim with rich storytelling language.

From Day One of kindergarten, many teachers begin reading aloud what Elizabeth Sulzby calls emergent storybooks (these books also become known in many classrooms as "star books"). This begins on the first day of school so that the books can be reread many times. Star books tend to be lively stories with rich literary language such as *Caps for Sale*, *The Snowy Day*, *Corduroy*, *Mike Mulligan and His Steam Shovel*, and *The Three Billy Goats Gruff*, to name a few. They also tend to have a repeating refrain or line that makes the story memorable (but not a pattern book), and the illustrations match the story page-by-page so that children can use them to anchor their reading. Sulzby recommends that an adult read each emergent storybook aloud about five times over the course of a few days. As you read these books aloud to your children, try to use your own best storytelling voice, and your students will emulate you. Use as much expression as you can, use gestures, and point to the parts of the picture that match what you are saying (and your kids will do the same when they have the book in their own hands). If you have read the books many times, your children will know these books well enough to "read" them during independent reading, generalizing all that you have taught them as they sit with their own copies of the books.

What happens when children have a repertoire of star books that they know by heart? The language from these rich literary texts begins to seep into their everyday language, especially when they are *story-telling* during writing workshop. Children have an understanding of what literature is, how it sounds, and what it looks like, and they begin taking small steps toward creating their own stories that look and sound like actual children's literature.

Foster children's storytelling abilities. Teach them how to story-tell from a meaningful object and give them the opportunities to tell their stories throughout the school day. Pratice storytelling as a class.

One way to spark rich storytelling work is to ask children to bring in objects from home that hold stories and to then tell the stories of memories attached to those items. You might model several language prompts to get kids started: "This reminds me of the time . . ." "It started when . . ." or "One time . . ." or "This reminds me of the day . . ." These prompts will steer children toward retelling an event, a story, rather than listing information all about the item or photo. You might think of this as show and tell, and it is not altogether different; just imagine twenty-five children all showing and telling simultaneously, each to his or her partner! Some teachers have found it helpful and enriching to have separate storytelling time outside of writing workshop, to allow for additional support for oral language. If children story-tell at the start of the day or just after recess, their memories will be fresh and easier to recall and tell in the form of a story. They'll become accustomed to spinning the events of their lives into sequential tales. Then, during writing workshop, it will be especially easy for children to think of stories they can capture on the page.

Not only will you want to read aloud rich literary examples of stories and invite kids to bring artifacts and photos to spark ideas for stories, but you'll also want to practice storytelling together with your class. Help children recall events the class has experienced together and to spin those events into stories (not written stories, but oral accounts). Of course, the events can be small ones. You might tell the story of how, during a shared reading, a little inchworm crawled across the page of the book or the time there was a fire drill, and the whole class went outside with the rest of the school. After such an event you might say, "I love to think back and remember moments like that, don't you? Let's all do that together. What happened first? Who can get us started by telling us just the first thing that happened? Then what? Who can tell us what happened next?" You will want to show writers that people take the events of their lives and shape those events into stories. On one day, you might teach students that you can zoom in on the important parts of what happened and tell the story of it. On another day, you might use sheets of chart paper to make a blank book, and you'll draw a picture on each page of the book to represent what happened, one page for each step of the story. You might ask the children, "What else should we add to the picture so that we don't forget all the details of what happened?" Invite a few kids to come up to the chart paper to draw some of the picture, coaching them to add in important details. Draw the faces so that they show how the characters felt, for example; or draw the arms and legs so that they show the exact actions of the characters; make sure to draw enough of the setting that it shows where the story took place. Once you have actually turned the class story into a book, you and the children can reread this shared story. In this manner, you will create a few stories that the class knows well, and you will refer to these as mentor texts—examples of the kind of writing the children will do.

You might also teach children to work in partnerships to rehearse and story-tell and listen to one another before they write. Certainly kids will be doing this on their own as well, but at the start this is a good way for partners to work through different parts of the writing process.

Guide students to story-tell and then draw and write with specific details, including who was involved, where they were, and what they were doing.

Of course, the important thing is not that *you* are telling and writing stories, but that the children are doing so—and doing so at a great clip. In a minilesson, you might, for example, refer to a shared class text to point out that writers can tell what happened first and next, and teach your children that they could do likewise. Demonstrate how to picture what happened, then say out loud what you remember, and then draw the start on one page before moving on to the next page. Along with this you might create an accompanying chart, "How to Be a Storyteller," with the steps listed, "First remember. Next tell the story aloud. Then draw exactly what happened. Then point to each part of your picture and say the story to go with your picture. Finally, turn the page and do it again." For short, you might write, "See it. Tell it. Draw it. Read it." Of course the "reading" is really telling a story to go with the pictures.

In drawings, you may want to teach children to show not only *who* the people are, but also *what* they are doing. Coach children to progress from frontal pictures of people floating in the air to profile views of people interacting with objects, their surroundings, and one another. Remind them to include themselves, because they are also a (sometimes forgotten) character in their own book. Then, over time, teach children to include details in their drawings: "What does *your* dog look like that makes your dog different than any other dog?" you might ask. And "You say you walked your dog to the park, but what is that particular park like? How did you feel as you walked your dog? Could you somehow make your drawing show not only what you did, but also your feelings about what you did?" All of this information will not only help to fill their pages; it will also feed their oral storytelling. Children will at first say just the bare bones of what they did: "I went to Grandma's house. I played." When you encourage them to add the setting, they might say, "I played *in her backyard*." Later, they can include details: "I played ball." Next, they can add their responses to what they did, or their feelings. "It was a great day. I had fun." Encourage your students to draw and label each thing that happens and to reread their drawings often to tell the story again.

Some of this will feel like reteaching of what you already introduced in the *Launching* unit, and it is. Remember, when you introduced these lessons in the first weeks of kindergarten, your children were brand new to school. In those first few weeks, some of your youngsters (perhaps many of them) drew for the sheer pleasure of making marks on the page or for the pleasure of going round and round when making a circle or the fun of going up, down, up, down, making lines back and forth. You'll spiral back around to many of the early lessons on representational drawing, and you'll find that now that your children have had more experience with stories being read aloud, and a whole month's worth of practice with the fine motor skills involved in drawing, the work they do will be markedly different than the work they did when you first taught these lessons.

Revisit routines taught during the launch of your writing workshop to ensure that students are working productively and efficiently.

For children to carry on with independence, you may want to also revisit some of the routines you introduced in the *Launching* unit of study. Observe your kids to determine whether they need instruction in these routines or simply little reminders. Certainly many teachers find it helps to continually drop reminders to kids about how to move to and from the meeting area quickly and directly and how to sit on their bottoms, hands to themselves, on assigned rug spots. You may also need to remind children to turn all the way to their partner when it is time to turn and talk and then, a minute or two later, to turn their bodies all the way back around to you when you say, "Eyes back here." Continue to remind students to put their names ("That's the first word you always write on your paper!") and the date (date stamps are a helpful tool) on their writing, to put their writing in their folders (perhaps kids will store finished pieces on the red dot side of the pocket folder, ongoing pieces on the green dot side), and so forth.

Above all, you will teach your young writers that they can be problem solvers. Consider teaching minilessons that spotlight a writer encountering and solving problems: "Ingrid broke the tip of her pencil. Do you think that when authors run into problems they just sit there and go, 'Help me, help me, help me'?" (You may want to make your imitation of a needy writer's voice sound like the little rabbit in the woods, squeaky and weak.) Then shift your tone, stance, and voice to show that in fact, writers are just the opposite. Answer your own question by saying, loud and clear, "No way! Writers solve their own problems. Writers think, 'I can solve this myself.'"

Of course, you'll support self-reliance not only through the minilesson but throughout the workshop. Every time children act with self-reliance, celebrate this: "Writers, will you look here for a minute? I want to tell you about the smart work Pedro did. Pedro finished his writing. But do you think he just sat there and said, 'Oh, no, what will I do now? Oh, no, oh, no.' No way! Pedro solved his own problem. And you know what he did?"

This kind of independence is crucial. When children are able to carry on with independence, writing or pretending to write as best they can, and not relying on you for every little thing, you will be able to move among them, teaching into their work. This means that your first goal—helping writers work with confidence and independence, at whatever level of work they can pull off—actually enables the next goal, which is for you to teach in ways that dramatically lift the level of what kids can do.

Avoid the "bed to bed" story: Teach students how to storytell and write about one focused idea.

Once your class is on its way, writing booklet after booklet, you may begin to notice that some children's booklets actually contain multiple stories: "I ate breakfast. I went to school. I went to my friend's house. Then I went home." This entry summarizes an entire day, instead of storytelling one focused event. Not to worry, for this is a good start toward storytelling. Congratulate your writers on how chock-full of ideas they are. In a minilesson, share an example of one or two such stories and say, "Wow! You all are full of ideas for stories now! In fact, I noticed that some of your stories have three or four or even five stories in one!" Then build on this: "Here's *another* way to get ideas. You can take one of the things that happened in an old story and write a whole *new* story about that one thing. Pretty cool, huh?" Demonstrate this by writing your own brand new story that stays focused on just one of the events from one of the pages in your original book. Recruit a handful of students to try this technique, and then read aloud a few of their newly focused stories in a share session, asking the rest of the class to notice the difference. Your children will see how telling the story of just one little thing that happened is much livelier and more detailed than telling a story of a whole day.

The next step will be to teach kids to pick just one focused idea from the start and tell just that one story. That is, you'll teach writers to tell the beginning, middle, and end, not of their entire day but of just one small thing that happened in a day—preferably, a moment or a few minutes, rather than a whole after-noon: "Yesterday, I kicked the ball. I passed the ball to my friends. I scored a goal." Some kids might want to write about their whole day and may story-tell like this: "I walked to school, and then I went to my class and we read and played and ate lunch." Or "I woke up, went to school, came home." Help these writers find a smaller focus by choosing just one of the several main events: waking up, recess, or playing with my brother. Teach kids that writers often choose the one event that stands out the most in their memory or the one that holds the strongest feeling. This way children can spend their time thinking and working on stories that hold meaning and significance.

You can also teach students to utilize their writing partners for this purpose. Teach your writers to listen closely to one another as they share their stories, so that they are able to notice if a story stays in the same time and place. You can utilize partnerships to give students an audience for the oral rehearsal of a story, to allow your writers to work together to gain a smaller focus in their stories. This partnership work supports most state standards that expect kindergartners to speak audibly and express thoughts, feelings, and ideas clearly to others.

BEND II: WRITERS USE WHAT THEY KNOW ABOUT LETTERS AND SOUNDS TO SPELL WORDS WHEN THEY WRITE

Teach students to stretch out words slowly, listening for initial and even ending sounds. Adding labels to drawings allows even the most emergent writers to add print to their writing.

The first bend in this unit emphasized the importance of attaching meaning to each page of the booklets in which kids are writing. As children recall a moment from their own life, remember it, story-tell what happened, and then draw it in detail, they are learning the first, most important thing a writer can learn: stories have meaning.

Now that your children are on their way to telling meaningful, detailed, rich stories, you can turn their attention toward getting some words down on the page. You might show an example of your own writing, without labels, and demonstrate that without the labels, it's really hard to tell who the people are! "Was that my brother or my cousin? Gosh, it's hard to tell. Maybe I should label them so that it's a little easier to make sense out of this picture." If the majority of your class does not write labels already, start by modeling how to listen and record initial sounds. Show the kids how you say each word very slowly, listening carefully for the initial sound with an alphabet chart on hand. "What's the first sound I hear?" you'll think aloud. "Oh! /t/ I hear a /t/. That's letter *t*!" Then write the first letter of the word next to the item in the picture that you are labeling. Write the rest of the word and move on to another word, demonstrating again how to listen carefully for the initial sound. Emphasize that the words are there to help everybody make sense out of the drawings, as opposed to writing letters just for the sake of it (although this can be fun and engaging and may be something that some of your children have already begun to do on their own).

Of course, if some of your children are just learning letters and sounds, they might not automatically know which letter makes the sound they want to record. That's where the alphabet chart comes in. You may want to give an explicit lesson on how to use the alphabet chart to figure out which letter to write down. Say a word slowly, listening for the initial sound. For example, "Mmmmom" for *mom*. "Aha," you'll say. "I hear the /m/ sound. But wait, I don't remember which letter to write! What should I do?" Pause to let your children think along with you. "Oh, I know. Let me find a picture that sounds like /m/ on the alphabet chart. That will show me what letter to write!" Study the alphabet chart, pointing to each of the picture clues that accompany each letter, until you come to the picture clue for M. Suppose the picture is a monkey. You'll say, "/m/ monkey. Aha! M! Here is the letter I need!" Sometimes it helps children to trace the letter on the alphabet chart with their finger, then write it onto the page before listening for more sounds in the word.

Use paper choice, conferring, and small-group work to support students at various levels of proficiency with letter-sound correspondence.

As children work on their stories, circle among them and ask any child who hasn't yet added labels to point to something in the drawing—perhaps the child himself or herself, in addition to the bike, the sun, the window—and to label those parts of the story. You can invite a child to say whatever it is slowly. "Say *me* slowly. What sound do you hear first? Say it again." And then, when a child has isolated a sound, ideally the first one, say, "Write that! /mmm/ Write that." Act as if the child can definitely do this. Unless you act as if all children can, of course, write, and nudge them to do so, you won't have the chance to see what your kids can do. And, of course, every child *can* write /mmm/, even if some write a lollipop or a squiggle to represent it. The writing that the child produces in that instance will give you an instant way to assess his or her letter name and sound identification knowledge. Once you know what each child can do, direct different children to different sorts of paper. Children who know a handful of letters and letter names (if not also sounds) can write with initial and final consonants, because many letter names contain the sound the letter makes (as is the case for *m*). This means that right away, a bunch of your children will be labeling their pictures. These children, who can label using starting and ending sounds, will be very successful writing sentences to accompany their drawings and should be steered toward paper with lines for those sentences as well as a large space for drawing.

A child might, early on, sound out *somersault* by saying the word, just like that: "Somersault." Listening to the child do this, you may think, "She is not ready to write *somersault*." You are right. But the trick is to *teach* that child how to do this work! So if she is not stretching out the word, hearing the distinct phonemes or sounds in the word, and then isolating the initial sound, it is your job to *teach* her to do this! If another child records only a first letter for a word, then you definitely know that with just a bit of instruction, that child can begin to hear final sounds as well. As children spend day after day drawing and writing, expect to directly teach into what they do. You'll teach individually through conferring, and you'll teach in small groups, and you will ask children to work differently after you have taught them. Your teaching will often end with phrases like, "From this day forward, whenever you write, will you remember to . . ." As you look across the work that students do at the start of this unit, and in the middle of the unit, you should see dramatic and obvious improvements in their spelling and their control of the conventions of written language. A child who starts the unit writing left to right, bottom to top, will end the unit writing left to right, top to bottom, and adding punctuation to boot! A child who begins with no letter-sound connections can, within a matter of weeks, use a dozen letters and sounds.

As in all writing units, the growth that individual students make will vary. If you have English language learners in the first two stages of language acquisition, before children produce English, help them acquire language by pointing to parts of their pictures and saying out loud what you see on their pages. You might place your finger on a part of one such child's drawing and say, "Look at your writing! Is this you?" The child will respond with a "yes" or a "no." Then you can ask, "Are you in the park?" The child may nod his head. Continuing your observation and pointing, say, "I see a tree. I see the sun. Look at all the flowers!" This way, children will have some meaningful language experience between the teacher, the words, and their own drawings. Additionally, this process can be a kind of scaffold for students who are reluctant to talk about their writing. Keep in mind that the guidance you offer students will in many cases look different as you move from student to student during conferences and small-group instruction.

Of course, you will not just assess what kids can do. You will also teach to lift the level of what children do and to show them what proficient writers do that they might try. Through lessons focused on one skill or another, you will be teaching them something even larger: the whole enterprise of schooling. You'll convey that at school, a teacher figures out something the kids can't quite do, but could learn to do, and then teaches that thing, and then the kids try it and pretty soon—presto!—they can do this new thing.

As you teach children to say a word slowly and listen to its sounds, each of your kindergartners will learn to grasp the principle that each sound (or phoneme) needs to be represented with at least one letter (or letter-like mark) on the page. This is foundational, and even children who do not yet have a strong knowledge of letter-sound correspondence can learn this principle. You will also see that in short order, with strong instruction, more and more of your children will move from using letter-like marks to using letters. Once you have begun some work with phonics and taught or reminded children of letter names, you will see them using their beginning knowledge of letters and sounds as they write. A child writing the word *coat* might record a *c* or a *k* for the initial sound. If he hears an ending sound, he might use either a *t* or a *d* to capture it. These sorts of spellings are expected for kindergartners.

BEND III: WRITERS REVISE THEIR WRITING, GROWING THEIR STORIES LONGER AND LONGER

Have students rehearse for writing by storytelling multiple times before they even attempt to draw or write. Restructure the independent work time of your writing workshop to build in partnership rehearsal time.

In this bend, you'll build on the oral storytelling you've already established and take it a few steps further. You might start out this bend by teaching your children, in a minilesson, a secret that many writers know: writers tell their stories over and over and over again. The more times they tell their stories, the better the stories become. "In fact," you might say to your children, "many writers tell their stories three or four times before they even draw any of the pictures or write any of the words!" Then, in the demonstration portion of the minilesson, you might invite one of the children to role-play the part of your writing partner. "Watch how I tell my story aloud to my writing partner, not just once, not just twice, but *three* times, before I start to draw my pictures or write my words." Your kids will enjoy this—more talking! And you'll be astounded at how much their stories improve from one retelling to the next. Not only does the content of the story become clarified, but you'll notice that many children tell their stories more and more fluently and more expressively with each telling. Of course, privately, you know that this isn't exactly true. Many writers *do* talk to others (and themselves!) to work out what they want to say, but probably not in the same exact way you will teach your children.

For the remainder of the unit, you may want to modify the routines for writing workshop so that partner work comes first, and then independent writing time. This will give your young storytellers time every day to rehearse their stories aloud with their partners before getting to work drawing and writing, which will be done quietly, mostly on their own. You might teach your children that even when they are working alone, they may want to stop and tell their stories aloud a few more times, to themselves, and then pick up their pens and begin writing some more.

Instill in students the habit of rereading their writing and asking themselves, "Can I add more?" Remind them of all the strategies they know for elaboration.

Once children are progressing with independence, storytelling, writing, and labeling to their hearts' content, help them add more to their stories. Storytelling again and again will help many of your children think of more to say, right from the beginning, and you might be content with what your children are producing, especially if, as a result of oral rehearsal, they have moved from one sentence per page to more, or from three-page booklets to five. But don't stop there! Any first draft writing will have room for improvement, and it is never too early to instill the good habit of rereading one's own work with an eye toward revision. You may teach kids that before they put their writing on the done side of their folders, they should reread it and ask themselves, "Can I add more to my story?" Teach children that "adding more" can mean adding to their pictures and/or the words. You might remind students that you've taught them to add their feelings by adding smiles, frowns, tears, and so on to their pictures. Or maybe you've taught writers to add in more about the place where their story happened or even to add an additional page to show what happened next. If you don't already have one, make a chart showing writers all the ways that you've shown them to add to their writing.

Teach students to compare their writing to an exemplar piece, whether it is a demonstration text or a text read and discussed for read-aloud, as a means of self-reflection. Use writing partners to foster this work.

As a part of rereading and revising their writing, you might teach kids to think, "How do I know that I am done?" Certainly, they can look at how many words they have on the page, especially if they are labeling. Writers can ask themselves, "Have I labeled enough?" or "Do the most important things have labels?" A great visual way of teaching writers to self-reflect is to show them how to compare their piece with a class shared story or a piece that you have written. These can serve as exemplars, pieces of writing that are examples of what is expected in the unit. With your class, you could study an enlarged, chart-sized exemplar and use Post-its to label some of the elements that your students might want to include in their own stories: detailed pictures, labels, sentences, and anything else you and your students notice. Looking at their own writing side-by-side with a class exemplar, kids can ask themselves, "What did this writer do that I could do?" Of course, you'll need to make sure that your writers don't copy the *content* of the exemplar, but rather add the same *elements* featured in the exemplar (the pictures, labels, sentences, etc.) to their own work. As your children do this kind of comparison work, they might say things like, "Our class piece has two sentences on a page. I think I want to do that too!" or "In the class story all of the pages have labels. I can do that in my pictures."

Of course, one of the most important reasons writers make revisions to their work is to get their ideas across even more clearly to their readers. To foster a sense of audience, teach children to share the stories they have written with their partners on a regular basis, especially now, in this part of the unit, to get suggestions of parts that could use a bit more of this or that. You might even make the connection to the work children do during read-aloud, telling writers that just as they talk about books with their partner during read-aloud time, they can talk about their booklets in writing workshop. For example, just as kids look at the covers of read-aloud books and think about what the book may be about, they can do the same with a partner's booklet during writing time. Just as children talk about the parts of read-aloud books they think are important, they can do the same as they read each other's booklets.

Inevitably, drawing these connections will lead children to see how they can add more details into their writing. Children might notice, for example (and if not, you can point out), that in the books you've read aloud, the characters talk. The wolf calls out, "Little pig, little pig, let me in!" Children can then think about who in their own stories might talk and what, exactly, they might say. Presto: children will need speech bubbles! Similarly, partners might discover that adding more details about what happens (in the pictures and in the words) can make some parts of their stories really exciting or more important.

Your young writers can also learn to offer their peers suggestions as a way of strengthening their writing. Ask kids to notice what's already on the page and then to suggest one thing the writer could add. This might sound like, "Let's look at this page. You have lots of pictures but no words. Maybe you can add labels." Or "You have a picture, but there is lots of empty space around it. Maybe you can add more so we know more about your story." Or "Can you show where *you* are in all of your pages?"

When you teach students to ask each other, "What is this?" or "What else can you say here?" You are teaching partners to help each other clarify their writing. Teaching kids to clarify their thoughts and ideas is highlighted throughout most state standards. Of course, you won't necessarily expect partnerships to be able to make such suggestions without some concrete tools. Scaffold this talk by displaying partner talk charts and/or small tabletop tools that provide visuals (maybe two faces with speech bubbles) and some key words or symbols to make the tool user-friendly for kindergartners.

And of course, as students revise, you might also want to devote a session to having kids assess their work against the Narrative Writing Checklist. If you've already taught the *Launching* unit, this will not be new to children and they should be familiar with looking at their writing for one thing at a time from the checklist. You'll of course want children to celebrate new achievements and set new goals for themselves as growing narrative writers.

BEND IV: REVISING, EDITING, AND FANCYING UP ONE SPECIAL STORY FOR PUBLISHING

Writers fancy up their pieces for publication in several ways, including adding covers and writing dedications and "about the author" sections.

In this final bend, children are invited to "fix up" and "fancy up" one piece of their writing to prepare it for the celebration. You might also show your young writers that they can make a cover so their pieces look like real books. You may want to teach children to write dedications or an "about the author" page to make their chosen story special and fancy.

Teach students strategies for editing their writing to get it ready for readers.

The very last step for any writer is to proofread, to edit, one last time before sharing the piece of writing with the world. "Proofread?" you might ask, "But my kids can barely *read* read!" Even so, there are a few things your young writers can check for to edit their work. For starters, teach your children to check to be sure that they have spelled their own name correctly, by comparing it against the name tag on their desk or on their writing folder. Teach them to check one letter at a time, from left to right, making sure they didn't forget anything. They might add their surnames as well, if they haven't already included them.

Additionally, your kindergartners can reread their labels, one at a time, making sure that the letters on the page look right and make sense. A child might "read" the word once by looking at the picture and saying the word that goes with it, but then the child might say the word again very slowly, stretching it out to hear all the sounds, to see if he forgot to write down any of the sounds he hears.

Of course, as children are doing this editing work, they might add even more labels to their pictures. Or perhaps they'll add page numbers, or they'll underline or make bold words to show importance. All of these small, word-level and sentence-level changes count as editing or proofreading. Your children can also use the "Language Conventions" portion of the Narrative Writing Checklist to make sure they have checked their writing for everything they know how to do.

Celebrate!

For the publishing celebration, you needn't do anything elaborate. Perhaps your kindergartners will bring a stuffed animal to school and then "read" the story to the stuffed animal. These creatures can become a listening zoo and work as alternatives to partners on any day. Some teachers suggest children roll their pieces up and slide them into paper-towel rolls that have been decorated into "story tubes" and then march around the room singing a song. "We are the authors, the authors, the authors, we are the authors that are coming to publish our pieces." The parade can end at the bulletin board, and each child can then tack his or her piece into the appropriate square. That is, publishing shouldn't require a huge amount of fuss! Of course, in the best possible world, the way to publish the writing would be to help children see their "writing" doing some real work in the world. In this way, this unit could come full circle.

Looking Closely
Observing, Labeling, and Listing Like Scientists

RATIONALE/INTRODUCTION

This popular unit serves three important purposes. First, it is designed to help children develop the foundational skills that will put them in good stead as they move from emergent toward conventional reading and writing. Prior to this unit, children might have been reading and writing "as best they can," even if that meant that they drew, told, and improvised exciting stories without really using many letters. This unit channels them to transfer and apply their knowledge of letters and sounds to labeling items and listing observations. You might say the unit positions children to focus on their reading and writing, pressing the pause button on the fast-paced plots of their narrative writing to write labels and sentences instead. Children, then, are able to take the time necessary to stretch out each word, listening not only to the first sound, but to every sound after that. The unit also channels children toward writing list books, pattern books, and books with simple sentences that will likely revolve around high-frequency words.

Then, too, this unit is designed to teach children that writing is not only a tool for storytelling; it is also a tool for learning about science. Writing is a means through which children can study and come to know (and eventually teach) about the wonderful world of science, recalling information from experiences to answer questions. This unit positions them to begin to work toward these goals as they notice ways they can write about the world around them.

Of course, a third reason the unit exists is because writing matters and because science matters. Providing children with opportunities to learn about rich, engaging content matters. It would be difficult to overemphasize how important it is for children to understand writing as a tool for learning in the content areas. Many children are enthralled by any chance they get to study bugs, trees and plants, water and rocks.

This unit provides opportunities to see that learning about one thing leads to learning about lots of other things. Writing about a shared research topic, such as trees, provides a supportive scaffold for young kindergarten writers early in the year. Young children, of course, are dying to know how acorns turn into oak trees, where animals go in the winter, and why leaves fall from trees. It is a very good thing, then, when children are not only reading words, but, as educator and philosopher Paulo Freire has described it, are "reading the world."

It is crucial that schools give children opportunities to learn about the world and to expand their background knowledge. It is equally important for children to use writing as a tool, just as it is used in the real world by millions of people, for organizing, holding on to, and making sense of whatever content they want to learn.

MANDATES, TESTS, STANDARDS

If you opted to assess for all three of the genre strands (narrative, information, and opinion writing) before entering this unit, then you already have a baseline. If not, then now is the time to do an initial assessment of what your children can do, as information writers.

The explanation for how to conduct this assessment is continued in *Writing Pathways*. Remember that this is meant as an initial assessment, so you won't be conferring or teaching into the writing your children do on this day, just observing and encouraging them to do the best they can. Plan to use one writing workshop to do this, though it may take less time than that. You may stop when most or all of your children have run out of stamina, noting how many minutes your class was able to sustain writing and making notes on individual children.

Once children are done, collect all of the pieces to see what was produced, and use the information on the writing rubric for grade K (which is aligned to world-class standards) to determine a writing level for each child. This will help you decide what to teach in terms of structure, development, and language conventions. This assessment will also help you determine the kinds of paper (how many pages in the booklets and how many lines of writing) to start kids on, as well as what to teach your whole class versus what to teach small groups or individuals in this unit, so that you can differentiate for the range of needs in your class. You will want to do a summative assessment exactly like this one at the end of the unit, so that you can compare what students were able to do before the unit with what they can produce after the unit.

Your goals in this unit will include setting children up to address most state standards for writing and speaking and listening, as well as a few reading standards. This unit will set them up to work toward these goals and will provide many opportunities for repeated practice. It is possible, even likely, that by the end of this unit some of your children may be producing work that is approaching—or even at—the end-of-the-year benchmark for kindergarten. This series offers several chances for information writing across the year.

Writing to learn about the scientific world, of course, is an important part of most state standards. In this unit, children will learn specific ways to observe and take note of the physical world.

Of course, like many of the early primary writing units, there is an ulterior motive—to teach important reading skills. As your children compose information texts of their own, they are in fact doing much of the work they need to do to meet most state standards for reading.

A SUMMARY OF THE BENDS IN THE ROAD OF THIS UNIT

In Bend I (Living Like Writers, Living Like Scientists), students will "read the world," collect natural items and create booklets of representational drawings with labels and, possibly, sentences, to capture the details with precision, while referencing nonfiction books when appropriate.

In Bend II (Making Books Just Like the Ones We Read: Studying Mentor Texts and Making Reading/Writing Connections), students will begin to study the work of mentor authors. They will spend several days, or perhaps a week, learning from these authors ways to create books that mirror patterned information books and, in some cases, create booklets with complex sentences.

In Bend III (Writing More: Adding Details and Information and Writing Phrases or Sentences), students will learn ways to revise. You will teach them that revision helps them elaborate and extend their thinking. Your class will take three or four days to revise several of their most prized pieces of work, moving between recording careful observations and including their own thinking.

In Bend IV (Becoming Researchers: Scientists, Make Connections, Predict, Have Ideas, and Compare and Contrast), each student will study one science topic, chosen from several possibilities, and will create books about the chosen topic. Children will spend the week making observations, labeling their diagrams, writing captions, and creating information books that demonstrate what they have noticed and learned. Some children might study pumpkins or apples, while others are studying coconuts and palm fronds. This bend culminates the strategies that students have already learned. Children will end the unit by publishing books they have written on the shared class science topic or on their own independent topics.

GETTING READY
Gather Texts and Materials for Students

In this unit, you will invite children to observe, collect, and study bits of their world. You will need to decide, first, what shared class topic your students will study together during the first portion of the unit.

Many classrooms choose to study trees and decide to adopt a tree of their very own outside their school building, to observe and study not just for this month, but across the year. This allows children to see firsthand how trees respond to changes in the seasons. You will likely want to bring in a few boxes of large zip-top baggies to school so that children can collect "science artifacts" (leaves, twigs, acorns, pine cones, and more) to bring into your classroom while they are on writerly walks. You may want to gather trays or some other container in which to store the items your children collect. We suggest you find books to read and reread on the topic you are studying. For example, we recommend *National Geographic's* picture book series on seasons and trees (*A Tree for All Seasons*; *Seed, Sprout, Pumpkin Pie*; and *Apples for Everyone* by Jill Esbaum).

To help youngsters assume new roles, and capture subtle details, you could supply them with blank researchers' notepads and colored pencils. Then again, you might just decide to give each student a clipboard. You may also decide to send these clipboards home so children continue to live "writerly, scientific lives" outside as well as inside the classroom.

Your students' writing materials will need to change and grow as their writing abilities increase. For the start of the unit, plan to provide booklets that contain at least a few lines at the bottoms of each page, signaling that children should by now be writing sentences, as well as labels.

As you teach your children to value and grow their learning by paying close attention to the world, you may want to read aloud books that celebrate this aspect of the writerly life. Try Byrd Baylor's *I'm in Charge of Celebrations* (1995) or *The Other Way to Listen* (1997). Joanne Ryder's books also illustrate the wide-awakeness you're trying to teach, as do Valerie Worth's poems, especially those in her work *All the Small Poems and Fourteen More* (1996).

In the second bend in the unit, the mentor text bend, you will highlight the way that little leveled books tend to go so that children can model their own little books after the books they read: gather up a few favorites, particularly a few leveled books on the topic of choice. You'll be highlighting some of the simple things these authors do that your kids could also do: writing lots of pages on one topic, putting a sentence or so on each page, using repetitive language, and so forth.

Plan Excursions

Throughout this unit you will take your class on excursions. On many of these, during which you will encourage children to collect objects to bring back to the classroom. These objects can become part of the collection of items under study. If these excursions take you off of campus (as some surely will, assuming you are studying plants or trees), then you will need to secure parents'/guardians' permission and you'll need volunteers to join you. Plan accordingly, well in advance of these trips.

Choose When and How Children Will Publish

At the beginning of the final bend, you will need to decide whether your students will be publishing books that they have written on the shared class science topic or whether they publish the books on their independent science topics. You might then decide to celebrate the work of this unit by placing children's books on display in the library, the science lab, or the science bulletin board. Additionally, since one of the main purposes of content area writing is to teach others, you may decide to invite another class, one that has not been studying the topic that your class has been writing about, to come for the celebration. This visiting class will provide your children with an audience of readers who are there to learn new information. Perhaps your children can present one or two of their books to a partner from this other classroom.

BEND I: LIVING LIKE WRITERS, LIVING LIKE SCIENTISTS

Convey expectations from the start: volume, stamina, and transference.

From the start of this unit, we suggest you encourage children to write in three- to five-page booklets. There is good reason for this; booklets of this length provide built-in encouragement to keep going, to write more than just one page or two. You'll also want to be sure that the pages in the booklets contain plenty of room for big observational drawings with labels (for students to write label books), as well as at least a few lines at the bottom of each page, to signal to children that they should by now be writing sentences, as well as labels. It's hard to emphasize the extent to which materials themselves convey expectations. They should always march a few steps ahead of children, like clothes to grow into.

Because most beginning writers write with big letters, they will need lots of space if they are going to write words to accompany their drawings. Some teachers even opt to use legal-size paper for this unit so that kids have plenty of space to draw life-sized diagrams of leaves (or whatever the kids are studying), and so the children also have room to write a few lines at the bottom of each page. Just as the presence of lines at the bottom of each page conveys an important message to your students about the expected volume of a particular piece, supplying students with tons of books conveys the expectation that they will write not one booklet, but a whole lot of booklets. One book a week would be far, far too little writing. Kids this age can write even more than one book a *day*! The more books your children write, the more opportunities they have to write words.

Certainly you will want to encourage your kids to start another book as soon as they finish the first. Ask expectation-laden questions: "How many books have you written so far today?" "How many books do you think you'll write today?" "How many books do you have in your folder so far?" Be sure to celebrate the high volume and stamina that this unit is sure to generate. What could be more engaging for children than working with leaves and twigs, acorns and pine cones?

This unit offers an opportunity for children to apply and transfer all that they learned from any previous units they have participated in. If a few children become stuck or aren't sure how to organize their writing across pages, invite them to problem solve along with you, saying, "Hmm, I see you're having trouble getting started. What do you think you could do first?" This is a higher level of teaching and thinking, the kind of strategic thinking emphasized in levels 3 and 4 of Norman Webb's Depth of Knowledge model.

Rely on partnerships and conferences to support independence and problem solving.

Along the same lines, partnerships are great tools for propping up individual kids to address and solve their writing challenges. Tell them that, during independent writing time, when they really aren't sure what to do or to write, they can whisper to their writing partner for quick help, then go right back to their own work. This sort of peer communication gives students valuable opportunities to try out the difficult task of identifying and naming writing challenges and gives them chances to brainstorm ways to solve those challenges. As these routines are built into your writing workshop, students should begin working with greater independence, allowing you to hold more conferences and pull additional small groups.

You'll also benefit from providing children with some structured partner time each day. Children's enthusiasm over the science artifacts will naturally incite partner talk. While not dampening their zeal, you'll want to gently guide their talk by encouraging them to use scientific vocabulary (*veins, stems, leaves, bark*) instead of vague language (*thing, stuff, it*). Some teachers find it helpful to allow for five minutes or so of partner talk after a minilesson and before switching to independent writing time. You can direct your partner time by saying, "Take a few minutes to meet with your partner to talk about what you're going to write today," allowing children to be excited (and possibly noisy) while they are gathering ideas from what their partners say, before turning their attention to writing a transition into quiet work.

It is predictable that a few of your children will jump from topic to topic, writing something different on each page of their booklet, or that some of your children will put all of their energy into their pictures, neglecting to attempt writing letters or words. Teach your writers to stay focused on one particular subject as they write—to supply information through words. Use your conferring notes as data-in-hand to keep track of the students who are not yet doing this, and meet with them in small groups to coach them into staying longer with one topic and adding labels to everything, spelling as best they can. As you confer with individual writers, try to figure out a theory for each of your children: "What kind of writer is this? What does he or she tend to do often (not just one time)? Is there a pattern in this child's behavior as a writer that I could teach into?" Build theories about your children to help you effectively confer with each one so that you teach strategies that will help them progress to the next steps.

Have students research the world through books, experience, and observation.

In a few of your minilessons you will teach children that information is all around them; as they study, they'll find themselves wanting to know more, and they can readily find new information in all sorts of places.

One of those places is the pages of books. Perhaps you'll teach a minilesson in which you read from the pages of a big book and then incorporate a piece of information into a shared writing project. Before long, your children will no doubt convince you to allow them to keep book baggies or book bins brimming with books, alongside their writing materials. You'll explicitly teach students how to draw on a combination of experiences, observations, books and other sources to answer a question.

Of course, adding books to the mix adds a world of instruction. "If you want to know the scientific word for the little lines on a leaf—and of course, you'll always want the scientific word—then this book can tell you!" The words will sometimes be long and hard to read, but your children will be able to figure out many of these using pictures and the vocabulary resources you will have provided during shared reading and read-aloud. You could teach yet more lessons about using academic vocabulary, encouraging children to not just copy the words they find in books, blindly, letter by letter, but to try saying each word slowly, perhaps clapping out the syllables so they can articulate it clearly.

Throughout this unit, make a point of praising children's inclinations to observe closely. Encourage kids to pick up bits and pieces, to put these on trays, to examine them closely, and to draw them with an eye for detail. Stop children as they work, holding up one drawing or another, and talk about the smart ways in which one child used shape and color or another used size to make an item look real. Make photocopies of some of their work in progress to hang around the room or display on a shelf or tape to a chart. Congratulate children publicly for spending extended periods of time on one single drawing, adding more and more detail to it. Ooh and ahh when a child fills an entire page with a drawing of a little acorn. That child has made a small item very big, and scientists (and writers) do the same thing.

Teach children to draw representationally—seeing and hearing more means writing more.

Whether you have given your students colored pencils or markers, the unit will begin with a renewed commitment to making representational drawings, this time with writers working especially hard to capture details with precision, just as scientists do. Teaching children to draw representationally is significant work; doing so steers them to conjure up a mental picture of a topic and then to capture that image, that idea, with fidelity onto the page. The effort to put life onto the page, with detail, is fundamental to the writing process. Encourage children who are tracing to notice and draw the details on their own so that their writing is a place to practice observation and representational drawing, with an emphasis on observing, thinking, and carefully reconstructing.

Of course, this is writing time, so any drawing that children do will be a prelude to writing—and that writing needs to thread through most of every day's workshop. This means that as the year unfolds you should see children writing for increasing lengths of time, producing more and more text. As always, you'll need to use your understanding of what your children can do to guide each child toward the writing that he or she should be achieving.

You may gather some small groups to remind children to make many labels. Teach them to say words slowly, stretching them out, hearing the first sound, recording the letter that matches that sound, then rereading what they have written, continuing on through the word so they hear and then record the second phoneme. As you do this, you will be helping those children draw on what they know about letters and sounds. Some children may still rely on letter names for their sense of the sound the letter makes. (This works as a starting strategy because usually the name of a letter contains the sound associated with that letter.) Some children will already be hearing and recording beginning and ending consonant sounds, if not all the phonemes in a word, and you'll want to teach strategy lessons to these groups of children to draw on their growing knowledge of letter-sound correspondence, known words, and visual information when they write.

Nudge groups of children who are hearing and attempting to record most of the consonant sounds in a word to write a sentence under each picture, but be careful not to overstep. This unit is not meant to be a "fill-in-the-blank" unit where the teacher provides all the patterns, and the children supply the missing words. The big idea in this unit is that children will invent their own sentences and patterns, giving them an insider's understanding about language that will support them in reading as well as in speaking and listening.

During read-aloud time, you may want to stop as you read and intentionally model sentences that begin with prompts that are helpful for writing about science. For example, you can plan ahead that you'll stop periodically as you read aloud and use sentences that begin, "I notice . . ." or "I wonder . . ." or "I think . . ." This accomplishes two goals. You'll be demonstrating talk that is accountable to what the book actually says (as opposed to allowing your train of thought to carry you away from the text), and you'll also be modeling academic language that is incredibly helpful throughout the school day. During read-aloud, when you stop to give children opportunities to talk about books, you can coach them to use these prompts in their conversations. Later, if children are stuck during writing workshop, you could refer them to the growing list of accountable talk prompts you have displayed on a chart in your room. Surely by now your children are familiar with the prompts, "I notice . . . ," "I wonder . . . ," or "I think . . ."

BEND II: MAKING BOOKS JUST LIKE THE ONES WE READ: STUDYING MENTOR TEXTS AND MAKING READING-WRITING CONNECTIONS

Teach students to notice the structure and craft of mentor texts and incorporate them into their own writing.

Throughout your day, and through the weeks, you'll want to read aloud texts that support the content of this unit: books about trees, plants, seasons; poems, big books, charts, and texts that you and your children have created together. It is likely that one child will make the discovery (which you'll then share with the class) that the books you've been studying together can not only be sources for answers and information, but they can also become mentor texts. You might say, "You know those science books at your tables? The books we've studied together? Marco just realized that we can write books just like these about our own topics! About leaves or trees or our walks outside!"

Before long, students will notice features shared by these books written by grown-up scientists; they'll point out that these books all have covers with titles that relate to their main idea, that all the books have at least one sentence and often more on a page, and they will resolve to do likewise. You can help students discover that some of their just-right science books are written in a patterned way and some contain a twist at the end. Naturally, youngsters will want to write in similar ways. You'll see children writing list books with one phrase or label per page: "The leaf. The stick. The bark." You should expect other children to write simple sentences or patterns like "This leaf is yellow. This leaf is red. This leaf is green." Again, the materials you provide will make all the difference.

One-to-one conferences will support this work. For example, you and a child could compare a leveled book from the child's own reading workshop book baggie with the one he is writing—maybe even simply counting the number of pages in each. If his own book is shorter than the mentor text, then the child could aim to write more by stapling on some extra pages to his book. This work, of course, can become the centerpiece for a minilesson or a mid-workshop or share session as you invite other students to engage in similar work.

Some groups of children might benefit from learning to write different kinds of sentences (complex sentences, with a variety of language structures and punctuation). You might teach your whole class to notice that sometimes the books we read ask questions. Suggest that some of them might try writing a book of questions or a book of questions *and* answers. Playing around with syntax will also give kids plenty of practice with a new kind of sentence, more options for kinds of books to write, and a new way to think about the science they are studying: scientists ask questions at least as often as they record facts. You can add both to the list of options they have thus far collected (that list now includes all of the structures you've taught so far in this unit: label books, list books, books with sentences, and now questions and answers). But beware of simply assigning kids to write question and answer books. Doing this will lower the level of thinking kids are doing. (Keep in mind Webb's Depth of Knowledge, which places greater emphasis on students' ability to transfer and apply what they have learned on their own, rather than simply completing assignments and following the teacher's directions.)

By now, you've done quite a bit of work around the acquisition and use of topic-related scientific vocabulary during read-alouds, shared reading, and science time. If your scientists are studying trees, their writing should include terms like *stem*, *veins*, *bark*, and *twigs*. If they're studying weather, than you would encourage students to use vocabulary they've learned such as *temperature* or *precipitation*. Consider adding scientific terms to a science word wall or chart during read-aloud, shared reading, and science instruction. Add the words one or two at a time as they come up in your reading and shared experiences. Write the words in large letters on sentence strips or index cards, as you would for your usual word wall words. Be sure to include a photo, drawing, or other representational picture next to the vocabulary words so that all kids can access them.

Guide students to reread their own writing, making sure that it is readable to every reader, themselves included.

As this unit evolves, be sure that more and more children progress from hearing the initial sounds in words to hearing and recording all the phonemes. Identify the children whose spellings indicate that they do not yet fully grasp that each sound needs to lead to at least one mark, one letter, and give those children a great deal of repeated scaffolding. If they practice making labels every day, with you providing the support for stretching words out and hearing more constituent sounds, they will soon graduate to writing sentences underneath their pictures. Your goal is that they write so that they can reread their writing, using one-to-one matching, and so that you can read their writing too, or at least long stretches of it. You may want to suggest that when children progress to sentences, they first simply write, "I see the . . ." If this seems like dull writing, reassure yourself that it is not dull to children. These students are on the brink of learning to read conventionally, and one of the most important things they can learn is the concept of one-to-one matching. Even when a child writes a text as mundane as "I see the green leaf. I see the red leaf," and then reads that text back, pointing at each word as she reads it, that child is making gigantic strides.

It will be important for you to encourage children to leave spaces between their words (and through this, to develop more of an understanding of the difference between words and letters). If children squish their letters together without leaving spaces between words, teach them to reread, making slashes where they might want spaces. Another way to accomplish the same result is to listen to what the child wants to say, and then repeat each word, encouraging the child to draw a line under the spot where each word will go. The writer can then touch each blank, saying aloud what he or she will write, and then record a word in each blank.

BEND III: WRITING MORE: ADDING DETAILS AND INFORMATION AND WRITING PHRASES OR SENTENCES

Teach students to elaborate by looking closely at what it is they are writing about and adding details about what they have noticed.

Teaching children elaboration is a big part of both inspiring and propping children up to write books just like the ones they read. As part of this, you will both help students write more information about their topics and also support them in strengthening their writing by adding new information and writing with details. You might begin by teaching children that writers revise to include even more information. As writers learn more and more about their topic, they go back to their old books and add in the new information. Often a writer will decide to do a whole new drawing, and perhaps this whole new drawing might be one that zooms in on one part of an object, allowing both the writer and the viewer to notice more. Scientists, of course, sometimes revise to add more detail using magnifying lenses. If you have any on hand, they will certainly fire up your children's enthusiasm, especially if you saved them just for this part of the unit. Even if you don't have magnifying lenses, you can make "zoom lenses" from three-by-five index cards that have a one-inch hole cut out of the center to encourage children to focus on the smaller details of a larger object.

If earlier you decided to teach groups of children to write list books, these may have read, for example, "I see the leaf. I see the acorn. I see the pine cone." Now you will want to teach them to elaborate—to think and write more. There are lots of ways to help children elaborate, the most essential being nudging them to talk about and write whatever they notice or think or wonder about an object. You can also teach elaboration by putting a spin on what scientists do. For example, you might teach children that scientists usually write what they see first, but then they look again, this time for more details: "I see the leaf. It has little holes in it." Of course, it is also important to teach children (if they are ready) to alternate between recording what they see and recording what they think; for example, "I see the leaf. Why is it red?" Children might also observe and write off of photographs in the same manner. This should nudge kids even further toward meeting most state standards for writing informational texts.

Guide students to use a variety of spelling strategies as they write.

When children are encouraged to write whatever is on their minds, they tend to become inventive spellers, tackling words fearlessly. This means that you will want to encourage any children who are writing with just one or two sounds to slow down and listen for more sounds. If you notice other children starting to record some vowel sounds, plan to spend a little time during word study teaching about how to use short vowels to spell. You may convene other groups to work on using known words to spell unknown words. All of this will be possible because children will be using their high-frequency words and patterns to write with greater fluency. Since many of their sentences will flow quickly, writers will have more stamina to spell the tricky words using increasingly complex spelling strategies. Most state standards suggest that kindergartners should understand directionality and that words are separated by spaces in print. For students who have lots of experience with print, writing from left to right and top to bottom will come naturally. Some students might need more prompting for directionality as they write. After a student writes a word you might say, "Where will you write the next word?" to get kids used to writing left to right and top to bottom as they write sentences.

As students learn new strategies and crafting techniques, encourage them to return to old books and make revisions.

Remember, as this unit progresses, children will be churning out a lot of little books. They will write approximately three a week, each with three to five pages. This means that when you teach children something new, you can encourage them to revise previously written books, adding whatever you've most recently taught to those earlier projects. If a child draws and labels for the first week and a half of this unit, and then you teach her to write sentences, she might go back and reread her existing collection, this time adding a sentence to elaborate on every page of her earlier books. If you teach another child that in addition to recording observations, he could also record his thoughts, and suggest that one way to revise is to ask questions, that child could reread all his books, changing "I see the leaf," to "What do I see? I see the leaf," or "I see the leaf. I wonder why it is green." You might also have students self-assess against the Information Writing Checklist.

BEND IV: BECOMING RESEARCHERS: SCIENTISTS, MAKE CONNECTIONS, PREDICT, HAVE IDEAS, AND COMPARE AND CONTRAST

Decide whether students should publish from among the writing they have collected thus far or move on to independent science writing projects.

So far, the emphasis in this unit has been on making observations, collecting information and details, and recording those details on the page through drawing and writing labels and sentences—and for many classrooms with beginning writers this can and should be the emphasis for the remainder of the unit. If this is the case for your group of students, an option would be to wrap up the unit with children choosing a collection of their work so far and spending the last few days of the unit preparing to publish those pieces. This write-up, however, presents another option, one that provides the opportunity for children to transfer and apply all that they know about information writing to science topics of their own choice. Rather than wrapping up now, you may decide to end the unit by allowing each of your children to study a science topic of his or her own and to become an expert on that topic to teach others.

Guide students to choose independent science topics to study, from resources you have made available to them. Remind children that they can apply all they have learned about writing about science through the shared class topic to their own independent topics.

By this point, you have read aloud quite a few books about plants, trees, or whichever science topic you have chosen for the unit. Now is the time to set up baskets of resources related to apples, pumpkins, snow, weather, the seasons, and any other science-related topics with which children should be familiar. Then, allow your kids to choose, from these topics, one to study. You may have a group of children studying apples, with real apples to examine, as well as books and photos to browse. Another group might be studying pumpkins, with a pumpkin to dissect with your help, along with seeds and some books about pumpkins. You'll probably want to get around to each group of children to teach into not only the writing they are doing, but also the vocabulary and information to go with their selected topics. You might read aloud to the group or do some shared reading or writing or simply have a conversation with the group. "Why do you think some apples turn red? What do you think is inside a gourd? How do pumpkins grow? And what does all this have to do with trees and the seasons? What is the same and what is different based on what we know from studying leaves?" Though a small group of children will be studying the same topic, they will continue to select their own ideas for each book they write. A child studying apples might write her first book about apple seeds, the next about foods made with apples, and a third about apple trees. Another child in that group, sitting at the same table, using the same materials, will likely write three completely different books, perhaps one book of questions about apples, another on how to make apple cider, and yet another on different kinds of apples.

Encourage your children to use what they know from the read-alouds as well as the science materials in front of them. Teach them that writers can also answer questions and write books based on what they know—not just about what's in front of them. So, for example, kids can write books that are about "picking pumpkins" or "how pumpkins grow" or "places to buy pumpkins" because all these are things that they may have studied this year or that they know from their own experiences. You might even make copies of the cover of each read-aloud book to make an easy-to-see list of all the books children have been reading about the topic. You may want to display the read-aloud books you've done in an easy-to-access part of the room, or even make a chart for each read-aloud book (as you are reading it, of course) to remind kids of the key content they've learned so that they can access that information during the writing workshop.

In many classrooms, the work children will do in their new topic-based studies will be the culmination of the strategies they have already learned. They will make detailed drawings, write lots of labels, and write sentences, and even patterns, using everything you have already taught—transferring it and applying it to a new topic of their own. They will have fewer whole-class shared writing experiences and teacher demonstrations to rely on, because they'll be studying a topic at their table rather than a topic the whole class is writing about at the same time.

Push students to think and write about science in ways beyond making simple observations. Science writers make inferences and ask questions, as well as compare and contrast.

For some classrooms, particularly ones where children are beginning to write sentences, it will benefit students to be pushed to learn new ways to think about the science content they've been studying. For example, you might teach your class that yes, scientists (and writers) do record exactly what they see in front of them, right down to the last detail, but they also can push themselves to think, "Why?" and "What?" "*Why* do leaves change colors?" "*Why* are pumpkins orange?" "*What* is the reason seasons change?" "What makes trees grow so tall?" Then writers can stretch their thinking even further by making a prediction (or hypothesis). Prompts like "Maybe . . ." or "Probably . . ." encourage children to hypothesize about the science artifacts in front of them, using all that they've learned up to now through read-alouds, science instruction, science walks, and so on.

Another option, either for small groups of children or for your whole class, is to arrange the science materials in ways that lend themselves to compare-and-contrast work. You might place a basket of different kinds of apples at one table, different gourds at another, pine cones and nuts at another, and varieties of pumpkins at a fourth table. Then teach your children that writers often look closely at objects to notice and record what is the same and what is different. Together, you might sort a basket of mixed leaves or pine cones or twigs, talking about what makes them each the same or different as you go—perhaps even writing at the same time. You might create a chart with your kids that lists some language for comparing and contrasting. "I noticed _____ is the same as _____." "They both . . ." Or "I noticed _____ is different from _____." "One has _____ but the other has _____." Then children can use that language to make comparisons related to their own topics.

As children become ready for more challenges, there is a host of possibilities. You can nudge them toward more precise words, braver words, or using comparisons to show what they mean: "Some apples are red like roses," or "The pumpkin is round like a basketball." You can extend what they do by encouraging them to question, perhaps even letting their curiosity lead to small experiments. For instance, the question "I wonder what is inside the apple?" will ideally be followed with possible answers (hypotheses). Teach children helpful phrases such as "Could it be . . ." or "Is it because of . . ." The scientist studying apples might conjecture that inside the apple must be seeds, and that could lead to an experiment (or in this case, a dissection, led by the teacher). This might be followed by, "What happens if we plant them? Will they grow into apple trees?" Chances are that you will not get to this work within one unit, but it will likely spark continued work around a shared inquiry, preferably one that brings fascinating items into your room—and takes your children *out* of the room—long after the writing curriculum has shifted gears.

Prepare for publication by rereading, thinking about audience, and fancying up.

As the unit nears its end, you may want to ramp up the rereading work that children are doing during writing workshop. Encourage them to use everything they know from reading workshop to read their own writing (to themselves and to partners during partner time each day): pointing to one word at a time, making sure that the words make sense, rereading to smooth out their voices. You can teach your students that writers reread their own writing again and again to make sure that it makes sense, sounds good, and looks right. Writers read with pencils in hand, ready to make changes as needed. Writers also use checklists to make sure their writing reflects all they know how to do, and you can bring out the Information Writing Checklist as children revise and edit their pieces.

Near the end of the unit, each child can pick one or two of the books they have written in this bend to revise and publish. As children prepare to publish their work, make sure that they have a clear sense of who their audience will be. Will their published books be on display in the school library? Does your school have a science lab or science bulletin board? Perhaps you'll invite another class to come and visit so that your children can present one or two of their books to a partner from another classroom. However you decide to publish, you can get the most out of this last part of the unit by reminding children that for the last few days, they'll be getting their writing ready to share with other people, real-live people, who are going to read their books. To prepare for this, they can add more labels, more words, more details, maybe even add color, a cover, or an "about the author" page to "fancy it up" and get ready to share.

Writing Pattern Books to Read, Write, and Teach

RATIONALE/INTRODUCTION

If you are about to embark on this unit, congratulations! This unit is just the thing for youngsters who are perhaps starting to "read" little books, the kind of books with short, simple, predictable sentences, the kind that go: "I see the bear. I see the tiger. I see the lion. I am at the zoo!" Or books that go, "Brown bear, brown bear, what do you see?" Some of your children might be pretending to read simple pattern books, pointing at the large print and saying the words by heart, while others may actually be reading independently. In either case, this playful unit, a favorite among favorites, is perfectly suited for them.

"Read?" you might ask, "I thought this was a writing unit!" The fact that reading and writing go hand in hand will be especially visible to your students during this unit as they work to independently author pattern books, which resemble the little leveled books you so often see in classroom libraries and in the hands of emergent and beginning readers. Students will build on previous writing units to use labels, lists, and sentences to make these pattern books. Many teachers rally kids' excitement for this unit by telling them that the pattern books they write will help fill the classroom library.

While the opening to this unit emphasizes making books and creating a more personalized library, this unit simultaneously sets children up to study and write with patterns. It's important, however, that you do not teach this unit in a heavily prompted way. For instance, we don't suggest you point out a pattern in a book and then assign all your children to mimic that pattern. While we believe that the concept of pattern books can be very supportive to beginning writers, we still want writers to begin with a content, with something to say. That is, for us, the meaning or main idea comes first, and then the pattern is constructed to fit with it. A child who wants to write about things she loves will construct a pattern that goes, "I love . . . I love . . . I love . . ." A child who wants to think, draw, and write a book about his favorite toys might instead construct the pattern "I see . . . I see . . .

I see . . ." or "I play with . . . I play with . . . I play with . . ." as a tool to showcase all his very favorite toys. That is, one goal of the unit is to encourage children to understand that writers make meaningful choices about how the text will go.

Consider the volume of writing that your writers are producing, and continue to build on that volume. You might do this by creating a little celebration ritual at the end of each week. Perhaps you will conclude each week of the unit by bringing newly authored books into the reading workshop, putting the homemade books into readers' bins, and inviting readers to read to each other books they created. Kids can celebrate the number of books they are adding to the leveled library.

You will find that your children will love seeing the books that they have written as part of the classroom library. It gives them a sense of real ownership and will absolutely ratchet up the volume of books that they write. Pattern books are also a big hit with children because once kids know the pattern, they have access to the book, which gives them a feeling of power as both readers and authors. By the end of this unit, your children will believe whole-heartedly that they could be the next Eric Carle, Bill Martin Jr, Beverley Randell, or Joy Cowley.

A SUMMARY OF THE BENDS IN THE ROAD FOR THIS UNIT

In Bend I (Writing Pattern Books), students will learn that their first priority in creating a pattern book is to come up with an idea or topic and then construct a pattern that makes sense for that topic. Then, children will find ways to use pictures and words along with the pattern to make books that people will want to read. At the end of this bend, which should last about a week and a half, each child will choose a pattern book (or two) to add to the classroom library for others in the class to read.

In Bend II (Writing Fancier Pattern Books), students will pay close attention to why an author chooses a particular structure, such as questions and answers, "see-saw" patterns, or twists at the end. In this bend, children will spend a week stretching themselves by writing longer, more complex patterns, often with more than one part. They'll reread often and work with partners to be sure that their text both makes sense and is readable to others, in preparation for adding these to the classroom library at the end of the bend.

In Bend III (Writing Pattern Books with an Opinion), students will create pattern books with opinions, drawing on what they think or how they feel about something. They might begin to show, not tell, their examples and, possibly, include dialogue to capture their opinion voice. This week will end with a final writing celebration, one in which students may give book summaries before placing their final pieces in the classroom library.

GETTING READY

Gather Texts and Materials for Students

To give your students models of the types of writing they will produce throughout this unit, you will want to show examples of lively, playful, engaging pattern books. Choose books that are simple enough that your students can learn how the pattern goes. The series, Brand New Readers, by Candlewick Press, is one you might consider using, as well as the Mrs. Wishy-Washy series by Joy Cowley and *Brown Bear, Brown Bear, What Do You See?* by Bill Martin Jr. You'll want to gather up very simple, repetitive patterns. Almost any level A, B, C, or D book in a classroom library will do. You will want to find books that readily highlight how the author sticks to a topic, organizes his or her thoughts across the pages, and uses high-frequency words, predictable sentence structure, and some examples that end with a twist. More complex patterns, such as *The Very Hungry Caterpillar*, *The Very Quiet Cricket*, and other books by Eric Carle, might be just some you choose near the end of the unit when you want to provide more challenge.

The paper choices you provide in the writing center should match the work that children have done in other units leading up to this one. Children could use full-page booklets, or you could make the books look more like the level A/B/C books in a classroom library—that is, booklets of half-sheets of paper. You will want the paper to have a picture space and then three lines underneath for writing. If students are filling the lines, then of course, encourage them to take booklets that have more pages than they will fill—in case they want to add more later. Always, you want to stay one step ahead of kids, encouraging them in one way or another to push themselves to do even more.

Choose When and How Children Will Publish

This unit is great for holding a celebration at the end of each bend to help keep energy and writing volume high. At the end of the unit, you might decide to have students give a summary of their books, so that other students may select the newly published books to add to their book baggies.

BEND I: WRITING PATTERN BOOKS

Create energy and excitement for the unit.

You might decide to launch this unit by creating a new space in your classroom library to hold the books that your young writers will soon create. Perhaps on the first day of the unit, you'll hold a little ribbon-cutting ceremony. Gather your kids in the library and gesture to the empty shelf. "Writers, you have been devouring books so quickly! The other day, I realized that you are reading so much now that soon we'll need more books in our classroom! And I thought that maybe *you* could make the new books! We can make the books for our classroom library *ourselves*! That way, our library can hold books about your favorite things—about your families and about your friends. Then it will be easy to find books you want to read because you will be the ones in charge of making them." Cut a ribbon you've stretched across the empty shelf and announce, "Today we will start writing books for our library!"

Teach students that writers first come up with an idea or a topic for their book and *then* think about conveying that idea with a pattern.

This first bend is all about creating energy for the unit. Your ultimate goal is to show writers how they can make pattern books of their own. You will want to be sure your message is that when writers create pattern books, they first think about how all the pages will go together to communicate an idea, a message, a topic, information—in other words, *meaning*—to the reader. Then those writers construct a pattern that will best communicate their meaning. In a minilesson, perhaps you'll demonstrate the steps of how one might go about getting started on a pattern book. First, you'll demonstrate thinking of a topic or an idea you really want to write about. For example, you might say, "Hmm, I love my dog, so I really want to make a book about him." Then you'll demonstrate how you can plan out the information you want to show across the pages, perhaps by touching the pages to say what might go there, and drawing a quick sketch. You'll touch each page, saying, "I want to show my dog playing, and on the next page eating, and on the next page chewing his toy, and on the next page fetching a ball, and finally going to sleep." After you've sketched and talked across the pages, you'll show kids how you figure out a pattern that make sense for the book. "Okay, on the first page I could write 'My dog plays.' Because that's what he's doing. The first page is always the easiest to write because the pattern hasn't started yet. Besides, I could always go back and change it. Now, on the second page, I want to keep the pattern going, because patterns are fun to read. So I can't just switch to 'He eats.' But I *could* write 'My dog eats. My dog chews. My dog fetches. My dog sleeps.' Yes! That's how a pattern works." After a quick demonstration, you'll want to recap that writers first think about the main idea they want to write about, and then they create a pattern by making all the pages go together across the book. Your goal will be to have most children finish a pattern book or two on the very first day of the unit. Approximately a book or two per day is how the pace of the unit should go.

Don't be surprised if there are a handful of children who have trouble connecting the pages of their books, who seem to simply copy your pattern or pick a pattern from a chart in the room or string together high-frequency words and fill in the blanks. The resulting text will sound odd: "I see a wall. I see a shoe. I see a pencil." What are a wall, a shoe, and a pencil doing in the pages of the same pattern book? These may be kids who are just plugging in words to a pattern, rather than writing a book that makes sense to the reader. Occasionally children (and the adults in their lives) are just so excited to be writing so many words and sentences that the lack of meaning is overlooked, and you'll want to watch out for that. Often it helps if students give their book a title early on, giving them a main idea to hook all their pages on to. It also helps to encourage students to plan all the pages out, by drawing all the pictures first, making sure all the pictures fit with the title, and then going back to write the words only after they've concentrated on the content they want to include in the text.

Highlight the key elements of pattern books.

On the other hand, you might find some groups of children creating books where the pictures all make sense and connect across the text, but the words don't match what the book is supposed to be about. For example, a child may write about her family, intending to have a page for each member of her family: "It has my brother. It has my sister. It has my cousin. It has my mother. It has my father." This kind of writing happens sometimes when children select a pattern to copy from a chart or when they string together high-frequency words, rather than constructing a pattern that makes sense. The child is focusing on getting words, any words, down on the page or perhaps feels limited to the examples that are displayed in the classroom. You might pull your class together to specifically teach them about making informed decisions with their patterns, saying, "Today I want to teach you that writers think very carefully about the pattern in their book. Remember that writers don't just throw in any old pattern. No way! Writers think about what they want to say to their readers and create a pattern that will make sense with what they want to say, even if it is a little trickier to write the words."

You should also point out how the picture on the page helps the reader understand the one or two new words on each page—the words that aren't part of the pattern. As teachers, we know that the pattern in a book involves all three cueing systems: meaning, structure, and visual. It is set up to help the reader use pictures to make sense of the book (meaning), to talk to the reader in a certain way (structure or syntax), and to look to the print to read the words (visual). You are not necessarily teaching the three cueing systems explicitly during this writing unit, but you want to make sure that your explanation of pattern books is balanced by these three sources of information. To help your children understand how to make a pattern book, you might display an enlarged example of a familiar pattern book, perhaps one that you have written together with your class, and then list some of the key elements on Post-its: a Post-it stuck right on to the title that says, "Main topic," Post-its stuck on each picture that say, "Ideas to go with the topic," perhaps a Post-it stuck to the patterned part of the text that says, "Words that stay the same," and another Post-it that says, "Words that change." If you label an enlarged pattern book like this together with your kids, it becomes an exemplar that you can refer to often to remind children of what to include in their pattern books, and you can add to the text with revisions and more pages, and more Post-its, as the unit goes on.

Expose students to a variety of patterns through read-aloud and shared reading time.

During this unit, it becomes tempting to try out a singular pattern and have each student write that "pattern of the day," but we encourage you to resist that temptation. There are several ways to avoid the pattern of the day. One way is to lean heavily on your read-aloud and shared reading times. You are probably already reading easy, engaging, patterned books in shared reading to teach beginning reading skills. When reading aloud, practice savoring the words: slow down your reading of the few words on each page; think carefully about the rhythm of the pattern and the stress you might put on each word. This reading tip holds true for reading your kindergartners' writing as well. You will want to model the savoring of their writing, helping all the children see the big beauty in these little books. To help your writers write with patterns, you will also want to make sure that in reading these pattern books, you are asking children to pay attention to how these kinds of books, levels A–D, talk. They talk with repetition.

In shared reading of these books, you will want to point out the characteristics of a pattern book. Think aloud and show, or invite your kindergartners to notice, things like high-frequency words, sight words, repeating sentence structure, punctuation, and the ways pattern books communicate meaning. You can talk about how the title holds all of the pages together and how it also might be repeated on the last page. You might show your students how pattern books often have a twist on the last page. This twist or "surprise ending" involves a change in the pattern and a slight change in the book's message. You will also want to highlight how the pictures in a pattern book don't just help support the words but add meaning to the new words on each page.

Getting children started: coming up with an idea, planning across pages, and recording pictures and words.

In this first week, as in every unit, you will need to remind your children how to find topics or ideas for the pattern books so that they are choosing topics that they know a lot about and that matter to them. One way to do this might be to remind kids of the books that they wrote in the last unit. For example, if your last unit was information writing, you can get the students thinking about how they might have used patterns to write about a particular topic. You might also remind them that they can write books about themselves. An alternative method to come up with topics could be by looking through the baskets of pattern books. You might teach your students how to look at the books in the baskets, thinking about how they might make their own version of the same thing. For instance, a child finds a little book about bugs that says, "Bugs are big. Bugs are small. Bugs have spots. Bugs have stripes." That child could think about how there are a lot of bugs in the park, and then he or she might write a "Bugs in the Park" book. It might sound something like, "Worms on the ground. Ladybugs on the slide. Flies on my head." You'll want your writers to think about the different topics or ideas that they might find in pattern books, so that they'll begin to realize what they might write about.

This will, of course, involve drawing pictures to plan how the books will go. You will also want to do some teaching about how the pictures on each page need to do two very important things. Every page needs to have a picture that the reader can search to find the meaning of the book and that also helps with the tricky word on that page. When students are drawing pictures, you will show them how writers ask themselves, "What needs to be in the picture for my readers to understand tricky words?" You could teach them that the writer is planting a clue in the picture to support the reader. You will certainly also be teaching that pictures in their books should go with the other pages. Second, you might want to teach how every picture needs to say as much as, or even more than, the words say. This supports making more thoughtful, deeper inferences. You might teach your writers to make sure that there is something, at least one thing, in every picture that teaches or shows one more sentence's worth of thinking—even though that sentence won't be written. In these early leveled books, pictures do all the work of encouraging reading between the lines, or inferring. You want your pattern book writers to help their readers do this kind of work in their pattern books as well.

Some of your writers will still be writing with labels, but in this unit you will want to show them how the label can go under the picture on the writing line. They would then be making level A books. These kids could be taught to do two-word labels on the writing line to help build their word-writing muscles. For example, if a child's book is entitled "My Toys" and his labels are "Balls, Animals, Cars, Games, People," you could teach him to add a word to help the reader know a little more about the thing on each page. The book might then go, "Bouncy Balls, Stuffed Animals, Little Cars, Board Games, Plastic People."

Differentiate instruction, based on what you know about your writers as readers.

You'll want to consider what you know about your children as readers and carry that with you as you confer in this unit. For example, children who read texts that are at levels A, B, and C and who are working on one-to-one matching in reading can be prompted to put spaces between their words, to reread their own writing, pointing under the words, to notice when they have left out a word and add it to their writing, and to write using first and last letters. These children can label four to six items on each page of their writing and can also be taught to write a sentence or two underneath their picture.

Many of your children's pattern books will be somewhere between six to eight pages long, about the length of a typical early level book that would appear in a leveled classroom library. In this first week, you are looking for your writers to write fast and furiously. Your hope is that they will have about five little pattern books done by the end of this first week of teaching, as increasing volume becomes a necessity and major focus. You will want to make sure that your children are increasing their writing output during each unit and across the year. If you think about it, these books are perfect for "fast and furious" writing because they are short and simple. You will want to make sure to tell your writers how many books you expect, and you will want to make sure that you model making that many too. Always remind them to use pictures to plan. Another thing to teach students to ask themselves when planning is, "What are the big things I want to say in this book?"

Sight-word writing and reading can play an important role in this unit, but you don't want your kindergarten writers to write books as if they were fill-in-the-blank workbook pages. What you don't want them thinking is, "I am writing about space, and I have to use these words on this list, so what do I say?" Instead, you want to show your writers how their own language, expressing their own ideas, can be made more patterned. You will want to be sure to teach children how to use patterns to express themselves. They can do this by taking the first thing they have to say about a topic and then thinking about if there is part of that first sentence that might be used on the rest of the pages. If a child says about a picture in her book, "This is a picture of a planet," then you want to ask something like, "What do you want to say about your picture?" She might say something like, "Space has planets in it." Then, the child could be shown how the rest of her book can go just like that first page. She would then draw a second page and talk out the words for that page using the pattern already established on the first page. Page two could have rocks drawn in space. The child could then write, "Space has rocks in it." Once your kids understand the patterns found in the books they read, you can teach them to change the pattern on the last page, as is common in level C and D books. To change the ending, you might show your writers how to reverse the pattern. For example, if they are talking about all the things space has, you might teach them to say what is not found in space. They might then write something like, "Space doesn't have me in it!"

Have a mini-celebration!

Maybe the last day of this first bend will have a mini-celebration. Your writers can take leveled baskets and then put their pattern books from the week in them or fill the empty shelf you cleared at the beginning of the unit with their pattern books. Partners could then read through the new "leveled" library books. What great reading work, and what great motivation to make more. You might say something like, "We have work to do. A whole class of readers is waiting for the book of their dreams! We have a library to fill!"

BEND II: WRITING FANCIER PATTERN BOOKS

Explore "fancy patterns" and think about why authors choose the patterns they do.

Until now, you've been teaching your young writers to construct simple patterns, the kind of books that repeat a simple sentence again and again. For a child who is just learning to read and write, filling an entire book with full, complete sentences is a thrill, and the fact that they can read their own writing, and that others can read it too, is pretty exciting. While these simple books are loads of fun for young children to read again and again, they'll also enjoy learning to make "fancy patterns." By now, you and your class have probably realized that playing around with patterns is a lot of fun. Finding the right pattern for an idea you want to write about is a bit like solving a puzzle, and writing a *fancy* pattern to suit the message in your book is like solving a more challenging puzzle.

Not all pattern books simply repeat the same line again and again. For example, in Bill Martin Jr's *Brown Bear, Brown Bear, What Do You See?* the pattern is a question and answer pattern. Many teachers play around with familiar pattern books that the class has studied as shared reading by creating innovations on the text. Instead of "Brown bear, brown bear, what do you see?" the class might create their own version, "Mrs. Moore, Mrs. Moore, what do you see?" This gives children the opportunity to transfer and apply familiar language to a new text. Then, if they decide to create their own question and answer pattern books (in the style of *Brown Bear, Brown Bear* or perhaps something more original), they'll be taking that language even further, on their own.

Whenever you are teaching kids about the different ways that books work, you will want to be sure that you talk about why an author chooses a particular structure. Different structures are chosen because they are the most effective way to communicate meaning in a book. During shared reading of lower-level big books, you might point out how some books have a seesaw pattern. One page goes one way, and the next page goes another. "I like ice cream. My mom does too. I like pizza. My dad does too." You might ask children, "Why do you think the author decided to use a seesaw pattern for this book? Why not make it a question and answer instead?" Then, of course, there are many possible answers to your question. Perhaps your children might say that a seesaw pattern makes sense because the foods "go back and forth" between the author and the family members. Or maybe they'll say a seesaw pattern makes sense because the text always has two things for each food, and a seesaw always has two sides. If your students have trouble coming up with possible explanations, you could model your own thinking and tell the children what you think about the author's choice. Then ask them if they agree with you.

You might want your writers to notice how some books ask a question and then spend pages answering that question. Perhaps an author might do this because he wants you to try to guess the answer before you read the answer pages, or perhaps the author wants to make all those pages of information feel more interesting by asking the question first. Or you could again point out that some books (particularly level C and D books) go one way for the whole book and then have some sort of trick or switch at the end. So a book about school might go, "We like to go to art. We like to go to music. We like to read and write. We like to do math. We like to go to gym." And for the twist, "We don't like to go home." You might share examples where the author uses the twist at the end because it's funny or because it shows the main idea or because it answers a question.

You will want the children to approach pattern books as writers, so that they are able to notice the moves the writer makes to make sense of the topic or story she is writing about. You will probably gather your students to teach them about making pattern decisions in their own writing by suggesting that they can study the different types of patterns that writers use. They can then decide which type of pattern would work best for the book they are writing, always thinking, "What would make sense?" When the children are reading beginning leveled books, we don't want them to think that all they are doing is practicing reading words so that they can get past these early level books and move onto the "real" books. They need to figure out what the books are about. The same goes for writing. We don't want our writers to write pattern books just to use words they know. We want them to be able to convey information, an idea or a story, in an effective way. Use compliments, mid-workshop teachings, shares, and student work on display to make it very clear to your children that you believe that even the smallest books can hold big meaning.

Teach students that writers use titles and endings in pattern books to convey meaning.

Earlier in the unit, you taught your children how the title often helps the reader know what the book will mostly be about and holds all of the pages together in the book. Now you might teach them it is a wise strategy to reread your writing often, checking to make sure all the pages fit with the title. You might show your class what to do if there is a page that doesn't fit. Take it out! Start a new book with it. Or if multiple pages do not fit with the title, maybe revising the title will fix the problem. You may want to take some time during one writing workshop to move from child to child, researching to find out if they are making books where all the pages connect to the title or main idea. If not, this will be a priority to teach in your next minilesson.

The title is just one way to communicate clearly. The ending is another way to convey meaning. It could say the opposite of the rest of the book and be surprising. There could be a big change or a new feeling on that last page of the pattern book. It could be all about an individual and then shift to someone else in the end, or it could be all about the rest of the world and then come back to an individual on the last page. You can teach your writers that using your ending to help a reader understand what you are really trying to say is what writers do in all kinds of writing. The Brand New Readers series by Candlewick Press does this kind of writing work well. For instance, in *Worm Is Hot*, the title does the work of saying one of the big ideas of the book. This book also has a surprising change at the end. You will probably need to collect and read aloud several of your own examples of books with patterns that do some fancier meaning work.

Teach students to use partners to ensure that their writing is readable.

In this second bend, you can emphasize the importance of partnerships in the writing process. The thoughtful work students are doing naturally extends into partnerships, because partners can help each other to make sure that readers are able to find the meaning in each pattern book. If a partner's meaning is hard to grasp, then the partnership is a great place to brainstorm strategies to embed meaning.

Students could also use their partners to help them make their books more readable. Talk to your writers about how they are writing for readers. What a partner can do to help with readability is to try to read a pattern book, and then the writer can pay attention to the words that are hard for the partner to read. The writer could then use those hard-to-read spots to help stretch and write words a little more conventionally. You will want to use your assessment of each writer's word knowledge—such as a spelling assessment—to help you teach the writing of words. Each child should be using what he or she knows (and what you know he or she knows) about words to help write the text in their books.

Continue to support your children in using several strategies to spell tricky words. Writing tricky words will inevitably slow them down. This is true in reading too. You will want to make sure that your writers are calling on all they know about how words work to help them write the one or two tricky words per page. At this point, you'll want to remind them to put down a letter for every sound they can hear when they stretch out a word.

Channel students to revise their pattern books based on the knowledge they have accumulated over the first two bends, and then celebrate!

This bend could end with another celebration of filling your library with students' writing, like you did during the first portion of the unit. You might have your writers work with their partners to transfer what they learned in this bend to their books from the first week too. This is really important revision work.

Because your kindergarten children have been writing label books or list books for two bends now, what they have learned should be showing up in all of their books. You could use your charts from both bends to help children improve all of the books they made in both bends.

BEND III: WRITING PATTERN BOOKS WITH AN OPINION

Teach students strategies for coming up with an opinion topic for their pattern books.

In this last bend of the unit, you are going to teach your children to write pattern books that express an opinion. According to most state standards, kindergarten students should be able to use a combination of drawing, dictating, and writing to compose opinion pieces in which they tell a reader the topic they are writing about and state an opinion or preference about the topic. So, since you have already taught your students that pattern books start with a topic, you can now show them how people often have opinions about a topic. You will need to teach your writers strategies for finding their opinion topics. Maybe you'll teach them to think about rules that they have to follow: bedtimes, rules at recess and lunch, classroom rules. Children often have strong opinions about the rules at home and in school. Show your writers how you might state your opinion by saying, "I don't like to go to bed early." Another strategy for getting ideas might be to think about the things they like to do, and especially things they like to do but aren't allowed to do all the time. For example, a child who loves to play video games but isn't allowed to do it all the time might use her pattern book to express her opinion, "I don't like anything except my games."

You could demonstrate how thinking about things you wish you could have or do can help you discover topics about which you have strong feelings. For instance, kids could think, "I really want to go to the Brooklyn Children's Museum," or "I wish I could have ice cream for dinner." Another possibility for ideas is that your writers could also learn to write opinion books talking about things that they like or dislike. For instance, a book in this genre might start with the idea, "I don't like to do laundry." So a book like this might go, "Doing the laundry is hard. It takes a long time. It is hot near the machines and it is hard to fold clothes well."

To make sure that children are learning to state an opinion clearly, you might teach them to say what they think or how they feel in three ways—in the title, as a beginning, or as an ending (or even all three). You might also teach children how to use a circular structure to begin and end their book with a clearly stated idea or opinion. No matter which structure you emphasize, you will want to be sure to teach your writers that these structures are chosen because they can help writers state their intended meaning most clearly.

Focus on Elaboration strategies for opinion pattern books: drawing, coming up with examples, and using dialogue.

It's possible that once children focus their attention on coming up with an opinion, they'll get stumped at that point. You may want to remind children how important drawing can be to help them say more about their ideas. For instance, if a child's book begins with "It is good to be nice to people," then he might draw a picture with one person being nice to someone who is hurt or someone else who is lonely. You could demonstrate how during your drawing you realized that you could use your picture to say more. You could then make a page that says, "Be nice to people when they hurt their knee," and another page that says, "Be nice to people who don't have friends too." Your writers could also use pictures to add more to their books than what's in their words. They might do this by focusing on the part of the drawing that goes with the words and drawing it in an up-close kind of way. For instance, if they say, "Broccoli is disgusting," then they might pull in close to someone eating broccoli, and draw his or her face with a scrunched-up nose and eyes.

To help your children write a little more in their opinion pattern books, you might teach them to help other people understand how they feel or what they think by giving an example. For instance, if a child's opinion is "Mario is fun," you might ask him to give you another sentence that goes with that one, hoping the child will say something like, "Yoshi is fun," or "The castles are fun." If you're tempted to steer kids toward a formula—by asking for reasons why Mario is fun—remember that examples can do the same work as reasons. Once children are giving reasons, or examples, you want to get them to show, not tell, the examples they are giving. For any one of the examples, they might just do some more explaining about that thing so that the reader understands more. You might say, "So, the music is fun. Can you say another sentence that goes with the fun music?" Then you can hope the child might say something like, "It gets fast when Mario is running and spooky when he is in the dark castle."

You might also teach kids how to use dialogue to capture their opinion voice. Teaching your writers how to ask other people how they feel or what they think about their topic is one way to get the opinion voice into their books. You could then show your children how you write down what other people say in dialogue bubbles and in the text as well. Children could also be taught how to talk directly to the reader to get the reader to understand their opinion. For example, "What you really need to know . . ." or "You are probably thinking . . ." can help them get their writing to sound more opinionated. You might also consider bringing the Opinion Writing Checklist into this bend, teaching children to check their writing for everything listed on the Kindergarten Opinion Writing Checklist.

CELEBRATE PATTERN BOOKS WITH BOOK SUMMARIES AND PLACEMENT IN THE CLASSROOM LIBRARY

As you finish this last bend of the unit, you will want to have a culminating celebration of the writing that your kindergartners have done across the unit. You might decide to allow students to share brief summaries of their books, so that others may select the newly published books to add to their book baggies. Not only would this be a great opportunity to empower your writers by acknowledging a true purpose for their books, but it will also help you to expand your classroom library, giving kids more books to choose from for their independent reading time. Of course, you will then need to be sure that the typed copies that go in their baggies have conventional spelling, since the kids will be rereading them multiple times. This will reinforce and expand their sight word knowledge, in addition to supporting other conventional spelling.

Writing All-About Books

RATIONALE/INTRODUCTION

Let's face it: your class is teeming with youngsters full of passions and areas of expertise. The child who knows everything about dolphins, the child who can tell you twelve million facts about makeup, the snake enthusiast, or the aspiring engineer who can tell you about each Lego set. One of the wonderful things about working with kindergartners is the delight they take in their own knowledge. This unit channels that energy into writing.

Kindergartners love being asked to teach you what they know and then to teach everyone else and the world. This means, of course, that we need to let children in on the fact that their beloved bicycle, their action figure collection, and their favorite topics—horses, insects, dinosaurs—are book-worthy! During this unit of study, each child will write lots of information books about lots of different topics.

This is bound to be a time of excitement as children reveal and explore their hobbies and passions, from playing soccer to raising a parakeet. You can help children develop new, important nonfiction writing muscles by channeling them to choose topics about which they have knowledge. There are topics your kindergartners know better than *you* do, more than their peers. Your young writers need to recognize that their own lives are full of so much that they can teach others. This is an excellent opportunity to tap into children's own funds of knowledge, to empower them to speak with authority and ownership about some aspect of their own life that is unique. One student may decide to write all about a sibling who has Down's syndrome, another may write all about life in a new country, and a third might write a guide to his or her neighborhood. The good news is that when any one is called upon to be an expert, teaching others, this fuels research. You'll find the child who writes a book about ants becomes even more observant of them. This unit, then, is about writing all-about books, and it is also about developing areas of expertise.

MANDATES, TESTS, STANDARDS

Before and after this unit, you'll want to do an on-demand assessment of your children's abilities to write informational texts. Follow the procedures outlined in *Writing Pathways: Performance Assessments and Learning Progressions, K–5* to do this. If you find yourself hesitating to weigh and measure your little ones in this way, trust us. Teachers who have used this method of assessing their kindergartners have been blown away by seeing what children can do and by looking at student growth through this window. You'll use the Information Writing rubric for grade K to notice what children can and can't yet do—and chances are that if you give children clear feedback, you'll see that many can approach first grade standards.

A SUMMARY OF THE BENDS IN THE ROAD FOR THIS UNIT

In Bend I (Writing All-About Books on Topics We Love), the emphasis is on organization. You will spend the week teaching kids how to stick to one piece of information at a time, rather than ramble on, and to make sure that all the pages of the all-about book fit together under one main topic.

In Bend II (Revise by Elaborating—and Then Begin Writing Longer Books, Right from the Start), kids learn how to elaborate and say more on each page. You will teach them to say more on each page by including more information, adding examples, and considering their readers' questions. They will also use many of the same strategies that they already learned for writing how-to texts. Plan to spend a week on this bend.

In Bend III (Revising to Add Text Features—Then Writing More Developed Books from the Start), students will spend the week learning to revise and also write new books, incorporating into their own writing the features of nonfiction that they notice in mentor texts.

In Bend IV (One Final Grand Revision to Prepare for a Publishing Party), the kids will pick one book to revise, edit, and publish for the celebration. This week will culminate with a writing celebration where students teach others all about their areas of expertise.

GETTING READY
Gather Texts and Materials for Students

You will also want to prepare for the unit by acquiring (or making) paper that can support your students' writing during the unit. Analyzing your students' on-demand assessments can help you make decisions about the kind of work you can expect your children to do in the unit, and those decisions will have implications related to paper choice.

You will also want to prepare Tiny Topics notepads for your students to use in the first bend of the unit. These can be simple notepads made from scrap paper stapled into small pocket-sized booklets. Or you may decide to purchase small notepads that can be attached to a lanyard, so that students can carry their Tiny Topics notepads with them wherever they go, living like writers and recording their ideas for new books.

You may decide to have five-page booklets available that resemble (or actually are!) the paper choice your writers used for narrative writing, with a box for a quick sketch and plenty of lines to fill with information (three lines or more per page!). In addition to booklets, you will also want to have plenty of stacked loose paper available so that, from the start, your writers know that pages and parts will be added because of all they know and need to teach. As you read through this unit, you will find that we do say more about types of paper choice and offer suggestions for how to use the paper choices to support writers. You'll also find suggestions for materials that will entice children to revise, including special pens, flaps, and brightly colored Post-its.

You will rally and renew your kindergarten writers' excitement about all-about writing by offering some spectacular new mentor texts. Choose texts that represent complex grade level texts, as well as mentors that are just a notch up from those that you expect your children will write. Make sure that the mentor texts you select will provide you with examples that you need to teach the content of in this unit. For example, you will want mentor texts with chapter titles, separate sections or chapters for each category of information, diagrams, and labels. Some questions to consider when picking a text are: Will this text support the volume of writing that I expect my children to produce? Will this text use elaboration strategies that I want my children to strive for? Will the text structure teach my children about ways to organize their writing? Some children may benefit from a list-like structure (similar to the books that they are reading), while other children will benefit from mentors with sophisticated text structures and elaboration strategies. You may turn to the nonfiction books in the National Geographic Readers series, such as *Trucks!*, *Planes*, or *Trains*, since these are nice examples of all-about texts. You may also want to refer back to the text you used during the *How-To* unit of study, *My First Soccer Game* by Alyssa Satin Capucilli.

CHOOSE WHEN AND HOW CHILDREN WILL PUBLISH

This unit is designed to have children write many all-about books on topics of their choice. Then they will select one to publish toward the end of the unit. Because the point of writing informational texts is to teach others, be sure to plan your celebration to incorporate this element. Inviting guests into the classroom will give your students an opportunity to teach all about their areas of expertise.

BEND I: WRITING ALL-ABOUT BOOKS ON TOPICS WE LOVE

Help students choose topics based on areas of personal expertise. Encourage them to also consider their audience when selecting topics.

Don Graves, one of the leaders in the field of children's writing, once asked a group of teachers to list their children's names. Then he asked the teachers to list, beside each name, four or five things on which that child is an expert. His point was that none of us can teach writing unless we recognize that each child in our class is an expert on many things. A child may know all about a specific church, about a game, about a tradition, about a sport, about a television show, about a kind of weather, about a place, about a job, about an animal, or about a language. These topics and a trillion others all merit attention, and the important thing is that you find these areas of expertise and respect them. In classrooms where informational writing will flourish, one will hear the teacher saying to one child and then another, "You know so much about . . . I'd love to learn all about it from you. You've got to teach me . . ." In these classrooms, children will push back their shoulders and stand tall, proud to be recognized as the class expert on one subject or another. It will not be hard, then, for children to choose topics on which to write all-about books. There will be instances when a child is unsure, however, and needing help. When you have the opportunity to steer a child toward a topic, we recommend that at least at the start of the unit, you channel children toward topics of personal expertise—and ideally, topics that will give the writer power as well. That is, a book on gym class may not give the young writer any social cachet, but a book on magic tricks or slugs or skateboard wheelies might, which will tend to make the young writer all the more willing to invest in writing in the future. We want children, as they think about their topics to teach others, to consider their audiences and to think about what people need to know and learn about in the world.

To help children choose topics that they will be able to write about with breadth and depth, you might have them brainstorm places, people, things, and topics that they know well and could teach others about (karate class, the grocery store, the Knicks, a Barbie collection, stuffed animals, helicopters). You could devote a portion of the first day to group discussions and partner work that aims to stir up topic ideas, and later, you might start the school day by asking children to suggest topic ideas to each other. As children wait in line, they could work with a friend to list five possible all-about ideas. As part of this, children will begin to recognize individual expertise. "Tonia should write about Littlest Pets toys, she has so many," one child might say. You may find that your students will begin working on books like "All about Sponge Bob Squarepants," "All about X-Box," and "All about Older Sisters." Don't project onto children the writer's block that you, as an adult, would experience if nudged to write an information book. Six-year-olds believe they are experts on a world of topics, and they expect that, of course, people will want to learn about those topics. On the first day of this unit, your children can start writing all-about books.

Introduce the Tiny Topics notepads as a means for children to collect potential writing ideas.

You might introduce the Tiny Topics notepads as something writers carry with them throughout their lives, the places they go, the things they do, and the people they know, thinking, "Hmm. Could *this* be the topic I decide upon?" and then jotting (or drawing) possible topics into their notepad. Be sure that you guide children to fill their tiny notepad with topics on which they have unique personal expertise and to decide, too, on topics that others would like to learn about. Soon these tiny notepads will be filled with sketches of their favorite toys and television shows and pictures of their friends, family members, and places visited. It will also be important for you to help children feel a sense of authority about topics they think are ordinary. If one child's mother just had a baby, that child may need you to help him or her realize that the rest of you would love to know what it's been like to have a baby in the family. If another child knows everything there is to know about the Dominican Republic, you may need to help that youngster understand that this expertise is precious indeed. Be prepared to be a student of your children, listening with responsiveness to any topic they throw out. There is nothing like a rapt listener to help us realize that in fact we *do* have lessons to teach and information to share.

After children have started to record possible topics in their Tiny Topics notepads, they may also want to think of an audience to go with each topic and a reason why they are writing for this audience. For example, one kindergarten writer insisted, "I want to write all about basketball for the people in the after-school program because I think they want to know how to play better." Another said, "I want to write all about cats for my friend Baylie because she does not have a cat and I want her to know about caring for cats like the one I have at home." When children know their audience and have a reason to write for this audience, they will not only have an easier time thinking of information to put in their books but also will be much more likely to compose texts that matter to them and others.

Getting children started writing all-about books: verbal rehearsal and planning chapters.

As children jot, select, and begin to write their first of many all-about books, it will be important for them to be given a few minutes to meet with their partners and discuss their topics. Just as they met with their partners to tell their stories or how-tos in previous units, children can meet with their partners to teach each other about their topics of choice. This verbal rehearsal will provide children with the opportunity to see if they have enough information to write a book on the topic, as well as to plan what it is they will write in their books. You may want to subtly guide your stronger writers toward more focused topics and your less strong writers toward more general ones. It will be easier to devote a book to the topic "library" than to "story hour," though that latter topic would probably yield better writing.

One of the most exciting and important lessons that you can teach your youngsters is that information writers sort things into categories so their readers can learn more easily. The simplest version of this is for children to say what they know, what they would write, for each finger, essentially writing sentences about each finger-topic. This might sound something like, "One thing that I know about recess is that kids get exercise during it. Another thing that I know is that a lot of kids play games like tag during recess." The children will be tapping their fingers as they ramble off information about their topics. Again, this rehearsal won't take more than a few minutes, so children don't need to wait to get started on writing chapter books. They can pick the topic they know the most about and start their books the same day! For this work, you can supply premade booklets with a table of contents page and a line on which the child will write the chapter title at the top of each page (for now, assume one-page-long chapters). Chapters may be titled, for example, "How to Take Care of a Cat" or "Parts of a Cat" or "Things Cats Like to Do." For each chapter, children will write what they know about that category.

One lesson you'll teach is that writers don't just throw everything they know about a topic onto the page in a giant hodge-podge. They write about one thing at a time. They try to write with some completeness about one subtopic before approaching another. In a minilesson, you might demonstrate how you plan out an information book by sketching just one important thing about the topic on each page of a booklet. "Now, when I write my words, I'll make sure that I say everything I can about my pictures." If you reinforce sketching and drawing *first* and writing the words *second*, you'll find that your children intuitively organize their content page-by-page. When they begin to write without a picture to focus on, they are much more likely to ramble, stringing sentences together that are loosely related. The pictures can help kids organize their thoughts. You could then point out that it might be hard for kids to remember things they are learning when everything is all snarled up together, and show them that people who are writing teaching books often sort things out and talk about things that go together, all at one time.

By now your children are up and running. They have strategies for getting ideas (especially by using their Tiny Topics notepads), and they know how to plan their writing by talking with a partner and by drawing the pictures first and then writing sentences to match the pictures. You might notice that the books your students are creating are similar to lists, that is, lists of information. This is an excellent first step to writing informational texts, and in fact this is what most state standards describe as grade level work for kindergarten. You may need to teach children to reread and be sure that their information is organized. For example, everything inside a page on dog food is, in fact, about dog food.

Expect that students will write with volume, producing many all-about books, writing many pages on each topic, and revising their books as they go. Introduce texts that can serve as mentors for the unit.

Remember that in this unit, children are writing *many* all-about books. They will pick a topic, make a table of contents, and then write their chapters. They will continue to revise their books as they go, like they have in every other unit. Make sure you have plenty of flaps and strips of paper ready so children can add information anywhere and anytime. Then they will start another all-about book!

Because your children will be writing many pages on each topic they try, you'll want to look carefully for texts that can serve as mentors for this unit. Using a mentor text like *Trucks!* by Wil Mara, you might show children how nonfiction authors hardly ever just write one little sentence about a topic, No, they try to write as much as they can, making sure that everything in the picture is also written about in the words. You might show children how a favorite mentor text includes descriptive sounds, colors, and specific vocabulary to add even more information to the book. In *Trucks!* there are special sidebars, or text boxes, that give a definition for key vocabulary words. Your kids might want to include this in their books as well. Remind your kindergartners that not only can they try this out in the book they are currently working on, but they could go back to all their old all-about books and add the new things they've been learning. And, of course, they can always start a new all-about book, this time using all the new strategies they now know.

It might be tempting, once you've discovered a few really engaging mentor texts, to show everything to your kids at once: headings, captions, sidebars, a table of contents, interesting punctuation, bold words, speech bubbles, and every other feature. You might want to hold back for now, focusing on the big goal of the bend, which is to get students writing one all-about book after another, making all the pages of their book stick to a topic, and making sure each page introduces one new piece of information at a time, so that the book presents information in an organized way.

Eventually, you may want to let children construct their own booklets and to at least expose them to paper written in different formats, because of course, diagram paper would be a good choice for a chapter called "Parts of a Cat" and how-to paper might be a good choice for "How to Feed a Cat." But, of course, both of those topics could also be written on any sort of lined paper, and most children will be more intent on plunging forward, writing a lot, than on thinking how a chapter will go and choosing paper to match.

BEND II: REVISE BY ELABORATING—AND THEN BEGIN WRITING LONGER BOOKS, RIGHT FROM THE START

Push students to write more. Encourage them to say more on each page by including more information, adding examples, and considering their readers' questions.

Every genre of writing has predictable challenges, and when writing information books, one of the most important challenges is to include information! This means that you will need to help young writers elaborate, or say more. There are lots of ways to teach students to say more. You might start by pointing out that now that your youngsters are writing books like real authors, they'll want to study what real writers do and think about doing likewise. One thing writers do, of course, is write a lot more than a sentence on a page. That is, they say more. That, alone, is great advice for your children. Part of this means that you need to be sure your expectations are properly high. If a child can write one sentence on a page, that same child can write two sentences. And frankly, a child can write two sentences on a page and four or five pages and do that in a day. Try challenging your kids. "Can I give you a challenge?" you can say to three kids. "I read that kids your age can actually write a whole book—like five or six pages long—in *one day*. And this person said those books can have a bunch of lines on each page. I think that's too hard for five-year-olds. I read that and thought, '*Really?*' But then I got this thought that maybe, just maybe, you actually *could* write a six-page book, with a bunch of lines on each page, in a day. Would you be willing to try? Just to see?" The kids will be bursting with excitement to show you and will rise to the occasion. And from that point on, your expectations for the whole class can leap ahead.

You can also lure kids to write more by teaching them that writers reread a page and think, "Can I add an example?" And then they get a giant colorful Post-it and add that Post-it onto the page, holding an example. Of course, there is no need for the Post-it. The example could almost certainly fit beneath the text just fine. But the Post-it will make the process of adding more feel like carpentry—and strips of blank white paper off the sides work equally well. Kids will enjoy folding the strips of paper to make flaps that open up. A writer who wrote, "Dogs are fun pets," may return to that page, reread, and then ask herself, "What more can I teach about this part?" Then she might add on, "Dogs lick your face. They will play all day with you." Keep your expectations high as you teach your writers to say and write more, and use tools to nudge your writers to reread and add on, as long as you also teach them that actually, writers write longer right from the start. In the end, if a child has written a chapter titled "The Parts of a Cat" and wrote only, "Cats have a tail," before he goes on to the next chapter, "How to Take Care of Your Cat," he will hopefully be able to say, "Oops! How can I say more about the parts of the cat? Well, cats also have pointy ears, four legs, and whiskers." You will want to be sure to make your own exemplar pieces extra long, so that you are modeling the same or even a little more volume than you expect from your writers.

Another important way for writers to elaborate is for them to consider readers' questions. By this time in the unit, your students will probably each have a folder full of four to six (or more!) all-about books. Teach children that they can read these to a partner, hear questions that the partner has, and try to write in ways that answer those questions. That is, if a child has said, "There are a lot of positions in soccer," then another child might reread this and ask, "What are the positions? Who plays them?" The author, then, can insert this information. You may need to teach children that they can use carets and arrows to insert information into the right spot in a text. Of course, the bigger lesson is that writers reread, asking themselves the questions that they anticipate readers will want to ask. They become their own partners.

BEND III: REVISING TO ADD TEXT FEATURES—THEN WRITING MORE DEVELOPED BOOKS FROM THE START

Teach students to add text features, with purpose.

As children continue to write multiple all-about books, you will certainly want to teach them that they can include text features in their writing, and again, you can use published all-about books as the source of inspiration. Encourage students to revise the books they have already made as well as to make new ones that include text features right from the start. Children can add diagrams, charts, glossaries, and pictures with labels and captions to their own books. They could even add a "Fun Facts" or "Question & Answer" page. You may revisit some of your favorite mentor texts to allow your writers to read with a writer's eye, noticing the features that the authors use to convey information. You not only want your writers to recognize what different features they might include in their books, but you will also want to teach them why they might choose a particular feature. Therefore, if you teach a minilesson on how to say more by adding a diagram, you will want to be sure to model how you decide where a diagram might help you to say more. You would not want to demonstrate that every all-about book has a diagram page, making students think that it is okay to just add in a diagram to any book in any old place. Instead you would want to teach your students several features they might add and how to go about deciding where to add what. Think about a child who is writing an all-about book on soccer, for example. If her first chapter is about practice, a diagram might not be the most useful feature to add. You want your young writers to begin to realize these types of decisions they need to make when they revise.

As you help children work on their writing, you'll want to be sure they use the skills that nonfiction writers use. You might reference the Information Writing Checklist, to be sure students are doing everything in their all-about writing that they know how to do as information writers. This will include incorporating technical vocabulary—the lingo of the topic—into their writing. Encourage a child who's writing about ballet to include words such as *plié* and *tendu*, for instance. "Look!" you might say, "In *this* book the author has made each difficult word bold and underlined and then explained it in the sidebar so that the reader learns what it means." Suggest that your writers do the same. "When you teach a reader all about your topic, this means *also* teaching the reader some *special words* about your topic." In addition, you might urge readers to elaborate on any subtopic by saying why a fact is important. "When you teach your reader about something, it might help to add, 'This is important because . . .'" Urge writers to reread their own writing with the eye of their reader, to think up the possible questions that a reader might have and answer these. Writing with descriptive details, adding number facts, and using comparisons to teach the reader more are also techniques that you might decide to teach your writers. You may want to create a kindergarten-friendly chart listing some of the elaboration techniques that you have taught throughout the bend. You can add on to this chart as the unit progresses and you teach more elaboration strategies.

Teach students that information writers write with voice, including their own thoughts and ideas about their topics.

You also might teach your writers not only to add text features, but also to say more by adding their own voice to their all-about books. For the child who is writing all about bikes you might teach him not only to state a fact, but to state a reaction as well: "Bikes have handlebars. You can put tassels on them. Tassels are cool!" A child writing about cats might write, "You have to keep the cat's litter box clean. Sometimes it is gross and smelly! Eww!"

You might work in small groups with especially proficient writers to help them know that when adding their thoughts about a topic, it can help to make comparisons: "Baby brothers are as fragile as an egg." Or "Sometimes dogs bark as loud as a horn. Those dogs are called guard dogs." Writers can also think about teaching through the use of contrasts, such as "Big brothers can drink soda and eat solid food, but babies can only drink milk and eat soft foods."

Expose students to a variety of crafting techniques that will help them teach readers all about their topics.

Continue to remind your kindergartners that their main goal in writing all-about books is to teach their readers all about their areas of expertise. There are a variety of methods to do this. Children can add warnings and suggestions in their all-about books just like they did in their how-to books: "Don't run up and pet a dog you see at the park!" Or "Be sure to inspect all the parts of your bicycle chain closely for rust!" They can also include features of nonfiction to teach more. You can teach them how writing under a picture—a caption—gives "ooh and ahh" information for their readers to learn even more. Or you might teach them how writers use labels and arrows to point out the important parts of a picture or diagram. You'll highlight determining importance, saying, "Do you think I should just label every little thing, or should I decide on the most important things that a reader should know about this picture?" Other features you may teach writers that will help them elaborate and teach more are the features of zoomed-in pictures and up-close details to both sketch and write. If you taught the "Looking Closely" unit based on the write-up in this book, students will be familiar with these techniques.

You might also teach your writers how to add an introduction to their information books as well as a conclusion. You can show them how an information writer introduces her book to the reader by asking a question and promising to answer that question as you read on. Additionally, at the end of information books, a writer often writes a big feeling or thought to leave their readers with so they will remember all they learned when they read her book.

BEND IV: ONE FINAL GRAND REVISION TO PREPARE FOR A PUBLISHING PARTY

Guide students to revise their chosen all-about book, using the elaboration strategies you have taught throughout the unit as well as in past units of study.

When children have collected many all-about books, they are ready to choose their favorite to revise further. Model your own excitement and enthusiasm for revision in your classroom. If you are excited to revise, your students will be too! You will want to remind them about all the wonderful revision work that they did in the previous units and build on what was previously taught. You might decide to revisit a chart on elaboration strategies in nonfiction writing created during Bend III and have students use it to revise their books. As children are rereading their all-about books, they could use the chart to suggest strategies for adding more pages of information and more sentences on each page. Children can also revise by thinking about what their audience would want to know more about or what their readers might be confused about or by responding to questions from a partner. They can also check for clarity by rereading their pages, stopping after each sentence to think, "Does this make sense?" and if it does not, changing it so that it does—or even taking it out. Children can revise their pictures to teach their readers more by "zooming in" on specific details or adding labels. Children can also study nonfiction texts and find new ways to revise their pieces based on what real authors have done, such as adding "teaching words" (e.g., *also* and *one way* and *another*).

As your class gets ready to publish, keep in mind that children will be making decisions on how their all-about books go together and how they will look. Urge your writers to study the external features of mentor texts to devise appropriate title and cover page designs for their books and perhaps create a back cover. In this prepublication stage you might even have partners read each other's books and write back-cover blurbs for each other, much as real authors do. One writing partner might read his partner's book about turtles and then write, "Read Eric's book and learn about pet turtles! ~Max, Age 5."

Teach students how to edit their books, rereading their writing multiple times, checking for one convention at a time.

Near the very end of the unit, your young writers will become editors, paying close attention to conventions, such as writing consistently with lowercase letters (rather than a mix of uppercase and lowercase), capitalizing the word *I*, and using simple ending punctuation and conventional spelling of word wall words. This will require careful rereading, with pencil in hand, and thinking about the readers who will soon be reading these all-about books. Your young editors will have better luck if they reread their writing multiple times, keeping just one convention in mind as they do this. You might gather small groups and guide them through the editing process of rereading their own writing once for uppercase/lowercase, again for word wall words, and once again for end punctuation. You might use—or adapt—the "Language Conventions" section of the Information Writing Checklist to do this work. Encourage your children to do this on their own. Even if they don't catch every mistake, you will still want to celebrate the work they are doing. The accuracy will come with practice and experience.

Students Celebrate by Teaching All about Their Topic

Celebrating this unit should be fun and informative. Because this is a teaching genre, it's best if your celebration can match this purpose. This is a great opportunity to turn your classroom into a Share Fair, since these books were written with the express purpose of sharing knowledge! Children will be proud of the books that they have authored. Your kindergarten writers might meet with another kindergarten class to teach them something new, or they might invite in older class or adults to tour the classroom as the children stay at "posts" around the room, ready to teach visitors about their topics. They might wear signs around their necks that say, "Ask me about cats," or "Ask me about bikes." This would be a nice way to celebrate the writing that your students have done. Remember to make sure that letting your children be the teachers is at the forefront of your plan!

Music in Our Hearts
Writing Songs and Poetry

RATIONALE/INTRODUCTION

Young children are natural poets. How many times have you watched a child tap her knees and chant lines of words to the beat? How many times have you seen a youngster spot a rabbit in the cloud or see swirls in the cement on the sidewalk? Young poets find significance in the ordinary details of their lives, draft with the intention of capturing life on the page, and learn from mentor authors. A unit of study on poetry, can teach children to write not only in that one particular genre but, also, to write better in general.

Across the unit, you will teach children to experiment with powerful language, to use line breaks, metaphor, and comparison to convey feelings. By the end of this study, your young writers will enjoy using both precise and also extravagant language to capture what they see and feel.

A SUMMARY OF THE BENDS IN THE ROAD FOR THIS UNIT

In Bend I (Immersion in Songwriting and Poetry: Setting the Stage), students will experience songs and poetry through their work in centers and through shared and interactive writing activities. It is during this week that students will get to experience many types of songs and poems.

In Bend II (Studying the Rhythm and Voice of Songs to Help Us Write Our Own), students will draw on Bend I in order to write their own songs. Students will begin to use tunes from familiar songs to jump-start their writing. They'll write lots of songs. Plan to spend another week working in this bend.

In Bend III (Songwriters and Poets Write from the Heart: Writing Meaningful Songs and Poems), students will reach for meaningful topics to write about. The emphasis will be on asking, "What really matters to me?" Children will spend this week learning to convey their thoughts and feelings through songs and poems.

In Bend IV (Songwriters and Poets Revise and Write New Songs and Poems), students will learn that poets and songwriters, like all writers, elaborate on topics they care about. In this final bend, try to make their best work even better, saying as much as they can and writing with careful attention to detail, in preparation for the ending celebration.

GETTING READY
Gather Texts for Students

To prepare your children for this unit, you'll want to read aloud lots of poems. Fill your students with the rhythms, sounds, and ideas of poetry. Help children notice how poems look on the page (e.g., line breaks and white space). Direct children to notice that poetry is not written in full sentences that march across the lines on a page. Poets use white space and line breaks to tell people how the poems should be read. Be sure to read a variety of poems to your children so they sense the breadth of the genre's possibilities. If you read only rhyming poems, for instance, then that is all they will write. Fill their heads with lots of different kinds of poems but above all, with poems that capture life's rich and beautiful details with precision. You will also want children to notice that poems can be about anything. Some tell stories, others are lists. You will also want to sing a number of simple songs with your children so that they have tunes in their head that they can rely on. Songs such as "Twinkle Twinkle Little Star," "The Wheels on the Bus," "Happy Birthday," and "Mary Had a Little Lamb" are easy to remember. You may want to write a class song through shared or interactive writing, sung to one of these tunes.

Some possible mentor poetry anthologies for this unit include:

Blast Off! Poems About Space, selected by Lee Bennett Hopkins (Harper Trophy, 1995): A collection of poems about space.

Creatures of Earth, Sea, and Sky, by Georgia Heard (Wordsong Boyds Mills Press, 1992): This is a beautifully illustrated collection of poems that express the enchantment of the natural world.

Good Luck Gold and Other Poems, by Janet S. Wong (Simon & Schuster, 1994): This collection of poems gives the reader insight into the experiences of Chinese American children. A variety of poetic forms are used, including rhymed poetry, free verse, and haiku.

Little Dog Poems, by Kristine O'Connell George (Houghton Mifflin, 1999): This is a collection of poems every dog lover will relate to and remember.

Songs of Myself: An Anthology of Poems and Art, compiled by Georgia Heard: This is an anthology of twelve poems and one traditional song about identity and the self.

Possible mentor songs include:

Songs to put you to sleep: "Hush-a-Bye Baby," "Hush, Little Baby," "Day Is Done"

Songs to show a strong feeling: "I Can See Clearly Now," "What's Goin' On," "Celebrate Good Times," "Oh, What a Beautiful Morning"

Songs to teach a dance: "Hokey Pokey," "Do the Locomotion"

Songs for people you love: "You Are My Sunshine," "You've Got a Friend," "Frère Jacques"

Songs that teach about something: "Wheels on the Bus," "This Land Is Your Land"

Songs that tell a story: "The Bear Went over the Mountain," "Itsy Bitsy Spider," "Mary Had a Little Lamb"

Mentor song books and compilations:

The Eensy Weensy Spider / Skip to My Lou, by Mary Ann Hoberman, board books with cassette (Megan Tingley Books, Little, Brown and Company).

Take Me Out of the Bathtub / Are You Quite Polite? / Smelly Locker, by Alan Katz (Margaret K. McElderry Books, Simon & Schuster).

Diez Deditos Ten Little Fingers & Other Play Rhymes & Action from Latin America, by Jose-Luis Orozco (Puffin Books, 1997).

If You're Happy and You Know It / This Little Light of Mine and many more . . . , by Raffi (Knopf Publishing).

The Itsy Bitsy Spider / Row, Row, Row Your Boat / How Much Is That Doggie in the Window? (and many more titles are available), by Iza Trapani (Charlesbridge Publishing, book and CD).

Follow the Moon / Without You / Angel Face (and many more titles), by Sarah Weeks (Laura Geringer/ Atheneum, book and CD).

Getting to Know You! Rodgers & Hammerstein Favorites, by Rosemary Wells (HarperCollins, 2002).

Old Macdonald / Mother Goose Songbook, by Jane Yolen (Boyds Mills Press).

Let's Sing about It! (songs & rhymes on chart, CD) Mondo Publishing.

Use Additional Professional Texts as Needed

When designing this unit, you might need to call on some inspiration and mentors too! You can draw on professional books, including *Awakening the Heart: Exploring Poetry in Elementary and Middle School* and *For the Good of the Earth and Sun*, both by Georgia Heard; *A Note Slipped Under the Door: Teaching from Poems We Love*, by Nick Flynn and Shirley McPhillips; *Handbook of Poetic Forms*, edited by Ron Padgett; *Wham! It's a Poetry Jam: Discovering Performance Poetry*, by Sara Holbrook; *A Kick in the Head: An Everyday Guide to Poetic Forms*, edited by Paul B. Janeczko; and *Getting the Knack: 20 Poetry Writing Exercises*, by Stephen Dunning and William Stafford.

Choose When and How Children Will Publish Their Anthologies

Poetry and songs are genres that are meant to be shared aloud. Perhaps you will decide to conclude this unit with a performance where other children can snap or clap their approval at the end of the show. Another possible option is to have the students record and burn their recordings onto CDs to share with others. A class compilation CD is a nice way to send home this work so that everyone can continue to appreciate all the hard work the students put into this their songs and poems.

BEND I: IMMERSION IN SONGWRITING AND POETRY: SETTING THE STAGE

Read and reread enlarged copies of poems and songs. Guide your students to notice the structural characteristics of these shared texts, and discuss the author's intentions.

Young children are natural poets. The poems they hear first and most often are the poems embedded inside songs. From the time they are babies, children are lulled or roused by the lullabies their grandmas sing to them, the songs they hear on the radio, or the themes that accompany television shows. Most children can recite the lyrics of a song before they are able to remember their own addresses! Think about how easily you recall the simple songs you learned in childhood. We all know "Row, Row, Row Your Boat" and "Baa Baa Black Sheep" by heart. There are reasons we hold onto these songs: they have catchy tunes, the words are repetitive, and they convey distinct, lovely images.

For starters, copy songs and poems onto chart paper and use these to read, sing, and teach a wide variety of songs and poems to your students. These "shared texts" will become integral to your unit of study. Once children know a song or poem by heart, then you might reread it, stopping along the way to say, "Huh. I notice that this poem has just a few words on each line, like the lines are broken apart. Let's call those 'line breaks.' Hey, I wonder why the author did that? What do you think? Turn and talk with your partner. Why do you think the author of a poem would break the lines apart like this?"

As children discuss the author's reasons for some craft move, whether it is line breaks or punctuation or repetition, you'll want to keep an open mind. Remember, there are lots of possible reasons why an author may or may not use a strategy. There isn't a right answer. The children might guess, "Maybe she did it to make it easier to read?" Maybe! "Maybe because it looks good, like it looks pretty." Also a great possibility. Of course you'll want to model ideas about the author's use of strategies that steer children toward thinking about meaning. You might say, "I'm thinking maybe she put these words together to show that they go together, as an idea." Or perhaps, "Maybe she set this word apart, by itself, to show that it is an important word."

As you launch this unit, spend a few minutes each day rereading familiar shared texts, noticing how songs and poems look on the page, noticing verses, line breaks, repeated lines, white space, and choices about punctuation, capital letters, and fonts. You and your children might notice that songs and poetry are sometimes not written in full sentences and that song writers and poets use white space and line breaks to show people how to read the poems and how to sing the songs. As you read these shared texts together, you might use Post-its to label some of the aspects of songs and poetry that you and your class notice and discuss together.

As you continue to study songs and poems with your students during shared reading time, you might stop along the way to discuss what the author may have wanted readers to feel. Then you might begin to slowly grow a chart of words that come out of these discussions—vocabulary for describing emotions and feelings. Of course, a chart like this is most useful to children if it is organized by meaning. Words that mean "happy," for example, might be grouped together at one end of the chart, while words that mean "angry" would be grouped together at the other end of the chart, with more words in between.

Continue to immerse students in studying songs and poetry through centers.

This reading work will probably occur during your shared reading time, separate from writing workshop. At the same time then, you might structure your writing workshop so that children have a chance to explore songs and poems close-up and on their own. Many teachers build students' excitement for writing poems and songs by launching the unit with a few days of song and poetry centers. Usually teachers organize these centers so each child and his or her partner rotates among centers, spending one day in a center.

Perhaps in one center children will listen to popular songs, songs they hear on the radio as well as songs they know from school. At this listening center, children may rely on a computer with headphones or a CD player. Either way, they will press play and then listen, and sing along. At this center, you'll have a tray of paper and pens available, and children will be encouraged to draw what they picture in their minds. Children then use their drawings about a song or poem to inspire their own song or poem.

In another center, children use instruments or tap pencils to keep the beat to familiar songs and poems. Get creative! Try to find rhythmic songs and clapping chants for this center. "Miss Mary Mack" and "Pat-a-Cake, Pat-a-Cake" are good examples. These children too, will be expected to write in response to what they hear, making their own poems or songs that carry the beat. In fact, you can say to them—and this is true—that this is one of the ways that many musicians get started when they are writing a new song. They have an idea for a beat or a rhythm, and then they make up some words to go with it. So, for example, children might sing and tap along to a rhythmic poem that you've taught them, like "Peas Porridge Hot." "Peas porridge hot, peas porridge cold, peas porridge in the pot, nine days old. Some like it hot, some like it cold, some like it in the pot, nine days old!" Then, they can make up new words to fit the rhythm, for example "Little puppy dog. Little puppy dog. Teeny tiny teeny tiny little puppy dog!" This may feel a bit silly, and some of your children will have fun coming up with nonsense words that match the beat or rhythm.

Of course, you'll also want to introduce children to the concept that sets poets aside from all other writers—their ability to see things differently. So another center could focus children's attention to look with fresh eyes at everyday objects: a crayon, a backpack, a chair. You can find poems that show children how poets see everyday objects with different eyes. You may teach children that poets see and then re-see and then see again, each time noticing something more. You might suggest that poets sometimes draw what they observe as a way to slow down and pay very close attention. Then, just as poets try to write about what they see and depict it in new ways, so too can the children write about what they observe and draw in new ways.

With your encouragement, children can begin to jot down notes about whatever they have been studying and drawing, trying to see these objects in different ways. As you sit down with children working at this center, you might say, "Wow! This feather reminds me of snowflakes falling from the sky." Then, demonstrate your enthusiasm for poetry by grabbing a piece of paper from a tray at the center of the table and show the kids how you can simply turn that idea into a poem. "Snowflakes falling from the sky," you might write, with line breaks for emphasis. Then you might turn to your kids and say, "What do you think of my poem? Do you think you could make one too?" For example, a child might say a stapler is like an alligator's mouth or a class plant is like a tree for ants. Young children are far better at this kind of inferential, imaginative thinking than many adults. They're accustomed to the world of make-believe and can easily pretend that a stone is really the moon or the clock on the wall is watching over us. Then, of course, you can teach kids that if they want, they can turn any poem into a song by simply singing it to their own made-up tune.

The list of possible centers could go on and on. In another corner of the room, children might be stationed at a window with a view, to practice looking at the world through the eyes of a poet or songwriter and recording what they see. Meanwhile, in another center, each child might read poems that contain strong imagery, such as "Turtle" by Charlie Reed, and then draw or paint what he or she sees in his or her mind's eye. You could invite children to join you in bringing in objects to use in a "five senses center," where they could practice using descriptive sensory language. In another center, children could learn to compare objects by using phrases including "like a . . ." or "reminds me of . . ." or "as a . . ." You might hang your children's paintings or sketches next to the poem they each illustrated, marveling at how one poem can provoke so many different images. In other centers, children could make shape poems or cut up poems to play with the line breaks. Another center could set children up to collect their favorite poems and to paste these into their very own poetry anthologies.

It might be tempting to try out all of these, but that isn't necessary or even desirable. Pick just a few, perhaps three or four or one center for each of the tables where children sit. Aim for centers that are based on your observations and assessments of your children's oral language, stamina for writing, and other goals.

If your children tend not to write much, choose centers where they'll be drawing and writing up a storm; if your children have trouble staying still for long during writing, choose centers where they'll be very active with singing and tapping out beats or moving around. If your children need help with writing with detail, you'll want to choose a center that supports that. The possibilities are endless.

BEND II: STUDYING THE RHYTHM AND VOICE OF SONGS TO HELP US WRITE OUR OWN

Ask students to look back at the writing they created in centers, looking for the songs that are already there or the words that can be turned into songs.

After a few days of song and poetry centers, each child will have collected a few drawings or lists of words or a rudimentary song or poem or two in his or her writing folder. These initial pieces of work will help them launch into the next phase of the unit: writing their own songs. You might decide to begin by teaching children that they can look back on all they have accomplished during their time in centers and ask themselves, "Did I already write a song? Or did I write an almost-song?" You might, in a minilesson, demonstrate rereading through your own writing folder, pausing at the end of each piece to say, "Can I sing this? Let me try." Of course, the resulting message will be that anything (almost anything) can be turned into a song. All you need to do is sing the words. You will want to do this with a pen in your hand, ready to make changes to the words that allow you to sing it more easily, so it rolls of the tongue a bit better. For example, perhaps you'll model reading a list of words you created by looking out the window and making an observation. You could read it in a flat voice: "Trees. Grass. Sky. Sun." Or you could read it like a song, stretching out some of the words, lifting and lowering your voice, making it sound melodic. Perhaps, with your pen in hand, you'll add some exclamation points for emphasis. "Treeeees. Grass! Suuuuuuun and Sky!" So, right from the beginning of the unit, your children will see that they already have begun to write songs. They just might not have known it yet.

Teach students to write their own songs by using the tunes and rhythms of familiar songs.

Of course, they can write more complex songs by studying the songs they know well and borrowing some of the musical qualities (the tune, the structure of the verses and refrains, and the rhythm in particular) to apply to their own songs. You might begin by teaching children to sing a familiar tune and then invent their own lyrics. Of course, it is not required that every child do this. They might decide to write their own poem or song from scratch. Perhaps some children will recall what they learned during centers, and they'll prefer to sketch and then make a list or write an observation. But it is likely that many of your children will be excited about this lesson. The aim here is for children to be energized by making favorite songs their own and creating songs from rhythms they themselves dream up. Imagine a child singing about going to her cousins' house to the tune of "Here We Go Round the Mulberry Bush" like this: "Here we go to my cousins' house, my cousins' house, my cousins' house. Here we go to my cousins' house on this pretty day." Children can write adaptations of any familiar song they know. For example, "The Wheels on the Bus" becomes "The Wings on the Airplane." "The Eency Weency Spider" becomes "The Eency Weency Sister" (". . . she climbed up the monkey bars"). Songs such as "Twinkle, Twinkle Little Star," "London Bridge Is Falling Down," "Happy Birthday," and "Mary Had a Little Lamb" have melodies that are easy to remember.

To support this work, you may also want to write class adaptations of these songs through shared or interactive writing, either as a class, or in small groups, especially with children who might need some extra support getting started. If some groups of children are hung up on making the words rhyme, a song such as "Frère Jacques" that has an easy-to-learn melody and lacks rhyming lyrics is a great early mentor for the students. It's a wonderful starting place for many children, because they'll have an easier time with word choice if they are not caught up in reaching for words that rhyme. Think of a child who writes, "I'm in the park. It's in the dark. There was a shark." Stringing together phrases that fit a rhyming pattern may be a starting point for some, but you'll quickly want to emphasize that writing needs to make sense if we want readers to understand our work.

Teach students to craft songs that teach and to write songs with purpose.

You might move on to study and write songs that teach something, such as counting songs, alphabet songs, how-to songs, or songs that contain information. In a minilesson you might sing a bit of the song "The Ants Go Marching," a counting song, and then demonstrate how you can take the same structure and tune to count something else—puppies, kids, anything. As you adapt the song, you'll stop to think, "Wait, puppies can't go marching down into the ground. That would not make sense. Where would puppies march to? Let's change it so our song makes sense." As a kindergarten teacher, you probably use songs for many different reasons throughout your school day, such as cleaning up, giving directions, and celebrating. You will want to harness the purpose for the songs that you sing in your classroom and pass them along to your students. Teach your students that we are inspired to sing songs when we want to celebrate, to give directions, to remember things, to tell about a feeling, to tell about an event, to tell about something that we want to have happen, to play a game, and any other purpose we have.

Some of your budding composers might prefer to tap out their own individual beats and rhythms from scratch. At each table, you might make rhythm sticks or small shakers available to inspire your children to try this out. They may tap their pencils, clap their hands, or play actual instruments. Once they have a beat going, they can use their creative sensibilities to come up with words. Some kids may go the other way around, writing out their lyrics and then adding a tune or beat that seems to match the song. Don't be surprised if children are tapping their fingers on their desks long after writing workshop is over or skipping and singing as they head home at the end of the day. Of course, it is not mandatory that every child tap out a beat to get his or her writing down on the page! As always, each new strategy is added to the growing list of choices, a repertoire that children can call upon when they are stuck and choose from as needed.

Teach other strategies for song and poetry writing, being inspired by objects and using your senses.

Of course, your children already know how to get inspired by objects to write lists or observations from their work during centers and other units, so another strategy is to look at or think of an object and let it inspire a song.

Have them close their eyes and imagine the soothing sound of rain on the window, how a tree sounds as it sways in the wind, and to turn those sounds into songs. As children do all this writing, you may want to give them paper that has been cut long, channeling them toward shorter lines. Then, all they need to do is sing it out, instead of reading it in a "plain old" voice. You might teach children how songwriters often repeat the important words in the list because this can accomplish two things: it shows the readers which parts are more important, and repetition can also give the list the voice of a song. That is, we don't usually repeat a word three times in a row when we're talking, but songs do it all the time.

Try to focus on keeping volume and stamina sky high, and keep tabs on each of your children to help them to be sure they are getting plenty of words down on the page, working with complete independence. By the end of this second bend, your children should be beginning to grasp that songs are different from other kinds of writing they have done, and their work will reflect this.

BEND III: SONGWRITERS AND POETS WRITE FROM THE HEART: WRITING MEANINGFUL SONGS AND POEMS

Teach students that poets write from the heart. Scaffold this work by having students write about topics that are important to them, using special objects as inspiration.

Ideally, your children are thinking, "Hey, this is easy! I can do this!" The first half of the unit scaffolded kids so that ideas for songs were readily available: objects to look at were right at their fingertips; familiar songs and poems surrounded them across the day, so that all they needed to do was list the words that came to mind, adapt an existing text, and voilà! A song! A poem!

Now, you'll turn a corner in the unit, encouraging children to reach deeper to find topics for songs and poetry that really matter to them. Instead of just writing about any ol' thing that comes to mind, you'll invite children to think, "What is important to me?" Perhaps at this point in the unit, you'll invite each child to bring in an object he or she cherishes—a special blanket or stuffed animal, a photograph or a piece of jewelry or a toy. Then you can teach them, in a minilesson, that they can fill their poems and songs with meaning by writing about topics that inspire strong feelings. Poets and songwriters dig deep to think about something they love and find the reason they feel such strong feelings for this object. The resulting song or poem could be as simple as "I love cookies so much because my mom bakes them for me."

Teach students that writers include strong feelings in their poems and songs and teach them strategies for showing these feelings.

Once your children are reaching deeper for more meaningful topics to write about, you might notice them struggling to find ways to show how they feel. You might see children, in their efforts to convey a strong feeling, using words like *very* or *really* (as in, "I really, really, really love my blanket."). Go ahead and compliment these approximations! After all, poems and songs like this are moving in the direction of conveying a strong emotion. As a next step for children who are writing this way, you might teach your children that writers have lots of strategies for showing strong feelings. And one effective way of showing their feelings about an idea or an object is to write a poem or song where they speak directly to the object (or person or place). For example, a child writing about his favorite toy car might write, "Oh, toy car, how I love you. You are always so much fun. You make me feel happy." Then, of course, the writer might imagine what the object might say back to him. As you move around your children during the writing workshop, you can nudge them to try these new strategies out. "Try it! You might like it!" you can say. "You can always change it back after you've tried it out."

Of course, writing to show a strong feeling is something your children probably know how to do from other units of study. You taught children to do this when they wrote personal narratives. You may decide to pull out the charts from past units. For example, a lesson from the *Writing for Readers* unit that taught children that the ending of a story could show the strong feeling could also be applied to poetry and songs. Children might even add a speech bubble to the picture accompanying the song or poem, and then that speech bubble might inspire an idea to add to the writing.

Poems and songs are meant to be heard! Build in time for students to work with their partners, sharing their writing and revising it.

Each day, before children write, you might give them a few minutes to share a song or poem or two with their writing partners. As they read to their partners, encourage them to read and sing with utmost expression. Coach them to use gestures and grand pauses, to lift their voice, and sing and read with feeling. As they share their work, encourage them to keep their pen in their hand the whole time, in case they want to make a change or a new idea crosses their mind. You'll soon notice children crossing parts out and revising their work completely on their own, simply because they had the chance to share it with an audience, their partner, and hear what their words really sound like when read aloud.

BEND IV: SONGWRITERS AND POETS REVISE AND WRITE NEW SONGS AND POEMS

Teach students how to be good poetry and song partners. Give them strategies for listening, reading, complimenting, and questioning.

By now your children are writing up a storm. Their writing folders are filled to the brim, overflowing with short little ditties, lists, poems, and songs. Probably most of these are one-liners with line breaks, a few words or a single word per line. At this point, your children have grasped (or are beginning to grasp) the concept that songs and poetry are different from other kinds of writing and also that songs and poetry hold meaning. Now you might want to nudge children toward writing a bit more, elaborating on their ideas. You will want to teach them to revise.

Throughout the unit, your children have been sharing songs and poems with their writing partners, and this will continue with renewed importance. Children's writing partners will fuel their motivation and enthusiasm for sticking with a poem a little longer, to add on, to take parts out, to revise. You might start this bend by teaching your writers that, as partners, they have two very important jobs to do. You might say to your young writers, "The first job, the job of being an active listener, has a few parts to it." Then, on chart paper, you might sketch two stick-figure writing partners. "First, you have to look with your eyes at your partner." You'll draw arrows from one of the stick-figure's eyes. "Then you'll listen very closely with your ears." You'll draw some arrows coming from the ears. "You'll probably need to point to the words along with your partner, too—to make sure he or she didn't forget anything." You'll draw a piece of paper between the two stick figures, with both figures holding the paper. Teaching your kindergartners to point along with their partner on their partners' writing is incredibly helpful for two reasons: they might be able to catch some of their partners' mix-ups on the page, but more likely, it will simply keep them more engaged and therefore make them better listeners.

"The other important job," you'll tell your class, "is to read your work to your partner so that he or she really understands what your song or poem is all about." The different ways that we sing or read our songs and poems give off different feelings and, thus, add to the meaning of our work. You will want to show your students that your voice carries a lot of meaning with it. "If I want my audience to appreciate the peacefulness or beauty of my song, then my voice will probably be light and soft, but if I'm warning my audience of something dangerous, then I'll sing in a sharp and, possibly, low tone." It's great to give students a chance in partnerships to sing their songs and read their poems in different voices, to see how each way communicates different feelings.

With partnerships going strong, you might teach your children that one of their jobs as a listening partner is to compliment the strategies that the writer is trying out. You might teach your children that they can use the writing charts in the room for ideas for compliments. Your young writers might need some language for complimenting. A few transferable talk prompts such as "I noticed that you tried . . ." or "I see that you . . ." might be helpful to model and coach into. The next step, then, would be to teach the listening partners how to support the writer. For example, children can use the charts in the room to make suggestions. They might say to each other, "Have you tried . . ." from a chart listing key strategies that you have taught. With a partner who is truly listening, it is remarkable how seriously young children will take their work. Don't be surprised if it is difficult to get children to put their writing away at the end of writing workshop!

As they've done in other units, partners will read together, offering each other suggestions about line breaks and white space. They might ask each other, "Why did you choose to add a line break here?" Partners could ask each other questions such as "Where is the big feeling in this poem?" or "What are you trying to show us in this song?" They will help each other think about their topics, the craft of their poems and songs, and the feelings they convey. You could teach them to ask each other questions such as "What small moment are you trying to rewrite?" or "Which writer do you want to be like?" Partners might also make suggestions such as "Have you thought of using this word instead?" Together, partners might play with language or line breaks to explore other ways a poem or song could sound or look to match the writer's meaning. Partners could even work to help each other come up with new topic ideas, either by revisiting the special objects that they began to use in Bend II or by reading through their Tiny Topics notepads together.

Teach students that writers revise through elaboration—adding verses, making comparisons, and thinking about word choice.

You can then turn your attention to introducing a few new strategies for lifting the level of the work your class is producing, chiefly by elaborating and adding more detail. By now, many of your children have hit upon topics that they are passionate about, yet their poems and songs remain the equivalent length of one or two sentences. If you read this ahead of time and are tempted to get their writing to be highly detailed and lengthy from the beginning, don't! The quick drafts at the start of the unit are quite intentional. This leaves their work perfectly set up for revision! If your children do too much revision, going back over and over their songs and poems from the beginning, they might not be as willing to revise at this point in the unit.

Show your children a favorite song or poem with multiple verses. Cover all of the text but the first verse. Read the first verse, and when you get to the end, you might say, "When poets and songwriters are writing about something they truly love, they often have so much to say about it that when they get to the end, you know what they often do? They don't just put down their pen. They don't just say, 'Oh! I love this topic. But too bad. I guess I'll stop writing about it.' No! They skip a line, pick up their pen and write another one about the same thing! A new verse!" Then read aloud the next verse, highlighting how it is still the same topic, the same piece of writing, just another part. Since your children are writing on sheets of paper with room for line breaks, many of them will now need multiple pages to make room for more verses about the topics they love most.

As children begin to reach for more to say about their topics, some of them will get stumped about what else they could add to their writing. You might teach your children to write with a bit more sophistication by using a comparison to show how the object makes the writer feel. For example, a child might write, "Cookies are like a big warm hug." You'll want to have read many songs and poems containing examples of this to your students. In a minilesson, you might practice the strategy of using comparisons by writing group songs and poems where children work together to compare an important classroom object—say, your easel or the lights, to something else. You'll be surprised to discover how many ways your students come up with to describe the lights: the ceiling is like the sky and the lights are the sun, shining down on us! You'll find that children love incorporating this technique into their own songs and poems. All of a sudden, a pencil is like a magic wand that makes things come to life! Compliment your children's approximations enthusiastically. Perhaps "I feel as happy as a car at a gas station" isn't the most majestic comparison, but it's a start.

While children are revising their poems and songs, you might also push them to think about language and word choice as a way to create clear images. They might explore the difference between *fry* and *sizzle*, *shine* and *sparkle*, *cry* and *bawl*. This work is all in alignment with most state standards around language. To guide your young writers through this work, you may find it helpful to choose a few mentor poems or specific poets and/or songwriters to study. These mentor texts provide your children with real and inspiring examples of how poets play with language and text placement to convey meaning. You could teach students how to create rhythm like Eloise Greenfield, line breaks like Bobbi Katz, or imagery like Valerie Worth.

Getting students ready for publishing by thinking about words, letters, and punctuation.

As children read and sing their work to one another, you'll probably find that is the perfect opportunity to remind them how changing a line to all capitals is one way the writer might let us know exactly how it is meant to be read or sung aloud. In partnerships, children might work together to decide, word-by-word, line-by-line, where it might make sense to write with all caps or a large bold font. In this way, children are thinking about conventions in a purposeful, meaningful context.

Additionally, you might teach into thinking about punctuation. When children read or sing aloud their work to an audience (their partner), it becomes more apparent where it might make sense to use a period for a full stop or an exclamation point for emphasis or perhaps a question mark when appropriate. Of course, songwriters and poets have options when it comes to punctuation. Sometimes a song or a poem without punctuation looks and sounds more smooth, like all of the ideas are more connected. Some of your young writers might prefer their writing this way. You might say to your children, "One way that poets decide on punctuation is to try a line with punctuation *and* without it. Then they decide which way is better." You might then demonstrate how you reread your own poem (perhaps enlarged on chart paper to make it easier to see) and try out punctuation, then take the punctuation out when it doesn't make sense to have it there. However your children decide to punctuate (or not), the bigger concept is to do so intentionally. That is, some poets don't just leave punctuation out because they forgot. They do it on purpose because it will add something to their work.

As children listen to each other's poems and songs, encourage them to listen to how their work sounds. "Does it sound like a song (or poem)?" they might ask each other. Of course, a little bit of repetition in a song or a poem can really lift the author's voice. You might teach the kids that a chorus holds the song together. You could also teach that many important words or lines in songs—sometimes called the refrain—are repeated. Children love repetition; it not only helps them recall something, but it's also a fun part of singing. Think about the pleasure of belting out the refrain, "Fa la la la la la la la la," or "Old MacDonald had a farm, E-I-E-I-O!"

You will, of course, continue to teach what makes for good writing and carry over things you've taught in previous units: details, the look of the poems, specific marks so others know *how* to sing the songs, and the importance of hearing and writing all the sounds in their words.

CELEBRATE THE POETRY AND MUSIC!

By the end of this unit, your students will have many, many little songs and poems bursting from their folders. At this point in the unit, you'll want to decide how many you'd like for them to publish. A few days before your planned writing celebration, invite children to pick a collection of songs or poems that they know they can read and can imagine performing. You might remind your children of a strategy or two for getting their work ready for readers, perhaps double-checking spelling and the spacing between their words. As children prepare for the writing celebration, they may reread their songs and poems aloud with a partner to practice their movements and intonations.

Poetry is a genre meant to be read aloud. Perhaps this unit will conclude with a poetry performance, a "coffee house" where hot chocolate is served and other children can snap or clap their approval at the end of the show! Or maybe you'll have kids make "albums" of their songs. Go for it! Let the children record and burn their recordings onto CDs for the songwriters to share with others. Children can celebrate by passing out lyrics and teaching each other their songs can be sung. Some teachers even hold little concerts in which children perform for an audience.

With a Little Help from My Friends

Independent Writing Projects across the Genres

RATIONALE/INTRODUCTION

Why do we write? There are hundreds of reasons. We write because we know that our writing can help us to accomplish something important. We write to share an important event in our life, to remember, to extend an invitation, to make people laugh, to vent, to teach, to argue, to persuade.

Skilled writers have a repertoire of genres in which they work, and they have an awareness of how each genre is its own particular tool. If you want to nudge your kindergartners to think, write, and draw as best they can in powerful ways, it is important for them to know that writers choose the genre that works for their purpose.

This unit will help set your children up for their "at home writing life" just before they are ready to venture into the summer months. This unit gives children a chance to choose from and practice writing in a variety of forms. This unit will breathe new life into your writing workshop, it will infuse genre studies with greater purpose and meaning throughout the month, and it will set children up to orchestrate all that they know to write with independence.

A SUMMARY OF THE BENDS IN THE ROAD FOR THIS UNIT

In Bend I (Getting Started with Writing Projects in a Range of Genres: Generating Ideas, Planning, and Drafting), students will self-select the type of writing that they want to study. Students will spend this first week recalling everything they know about that genre of writing to help guide them to generate ideas, plan, and draft. Students who are working in the same genre will band together with others working in the same genre, creating publishing houses that offer genre-specific support. As the month progresses, your students may want to try out different genres, and so the publishing houses will come to include both writers who are now "experienced" in that genre and writers who are newer to it.

In Bend II (Lifting the Quality of Writing), students will focus on the habits, processes, and qualities of good writing within the specific genre in which they are writing, to help them lift the level of their work. They will also turn to partnerships within their publishing house. They'll revise in ways that strengthen their writing. Plan to spend a week in Bend II.

In Bend III (Using Mentor Texts as Our Personal Writing Teachers), students will use the strategy of consulting mentor texts as writing teachers to further strengthen their writing. They will spend a week reading these texts in search of parts that resonate with them, study those parts closely to understand what the author has done to achieve a particular effect, and then attempt to replicate those techniques to raise the quality of their own work.

In Bend IV (Preparing for Publication), students will continue with independence, selecting a piece for publishing and thinking about what that piece really needs to make it the best that it can be. Then, independently and within a partnership, students will edit their pieces, paying close attention to conventions and spelling. This week will end with a writing celebration.

GETTING READY
Gather Texts for Students

If there are genres that are new to your children, you may want to consider reading some selections for read-aloud several days before the official launching of the unit. You may want to compile (or recruit children to compile) a few examples of a wide variety of genres. For example, you might want to show youngsters that writers can make any of these (or others) kinds of text:

- Narratives
- Picture books
- Song books
- Poetry
- Informational books
- Persuasive letters and reviews
- Posters
- Pamphlets
- Signs
- Cards, thank-you notes, friendly letters

USE ADDITIONAL PROFESSIONAL TEXTS AND STUDENT WORK AS NEEDED

You may also want to consult professional resources and draw on the work of the children in your classroom. Workshop teaching is most powerful when you respond and teach to your kids' successes and struggles. Because your students have had the opportunity to write in many, if not all, of the genres that you are including in this final unit, you may want to go back and consult the writing that they have generated throughout the year. By being attentive to student work, you'll be able to fine-tune your teaching. The work your students do is not just showing you what they can or can't do; it is also showing you what you can do. You could also look to *Independent Writing* by Colleen Cruz (2004) and *Assessing Writers* by Carl Anderson (2005) as additional professional resources.

CHOOSE WHEN AND HOW CHILDREN WILL PUBLISH

Assuming this will be the final publishing ceremony of the entire year, you'll probably want it to be a big deal. You may want to display children's work in a "museum" of writing. Displays could include evidence of children's process, along with their published pieces. Children can explain their choices of genre and publication to visitors. Another idea is to set up a "bookstore" with separate sections for each genre. There could be an area for author readings and posters advertising, "Meet the Author." However you decide to celebrate, you will want to make time for children to reflect on what they have learned about themselves as writers and to make goals for the summer.

BEND I: GETTING STARTED WITH WRITING PROJECTS IN A RANGE OF GENRES: GENERATING IDEAS, PLANNING, AND DRAFTING

Create a drumroll around independent writing projects and genre choice. Create genre-based small groups for students to work in.

Gather your youngsters together and tell them that for the upcoming month, they'll have a chance to invent their own writing projects. This is a departure from what you've been doing with children all year, and it's a significant step toward independence for your little ones. You'll want to create a big drumroll. You might say something like, "All year, I've been setting you up to do one kind of writing or another, right? Well, guess what? Now it is *your* turn to decide. It's *your* turn to come up with your own ideas for the sort of writing you'd like to do. The end of our year together is just a few weeks away, and for the rest of the school year, each one of you will get to pick the kind of writing you want to work on for the rest of kindergarten!"

Once children have decided on the kind of writing they want to make, you can channel them into different publishing houses, or writing clubs, with each publishing house representing one kind of genre. So all kids writing narratives will form a narrative publishing house, all kids writing poems will form a poetry publishing house, all kids writing persuasive texts will form a persuasive text publishing house, and so on. In their publishing house, children will be working side by side with others to make high-quality writing in the genre of their choice, sitting at the same table, sharing mentor texts, and giving each other tips to make their writing stronger.

Consider guiding students in their genre choices, as well as making sure that they are choosing topics that are within their realm of experience and knowledge.

Before you issue this invitation, think a bit about the choices you hope children will make because, of course, it is easy to steer them, if you so choose. Do you hope children will reflect on all the kinds of writing you have studied together and select one of those kinds of writing? Or do you hope children will pore over texts that they find in their world, thinking, "I could write just like that!"? It is possible for them to write adaptations of the types of texts they find most fascinating. Some of your students might be fans of *Dora the Explorer*, *Cars* the movie, or the *Toy Story* movies. Other children may be huge fans of superheroes or love to hear fairy tales and magical fantasy stories. They could write those, too! Do you hope some children will take on a cause—say, convincing the school to spruce up the playground—and that they will write to make a real-world difference? There are many possibilities, even ones your children may not consider without your guidance. Therefore, take some time to think through your priorities and imagine all the options. Of course, just because you hope children will gravitate toward your genre choices for them doesn't mean that they won't have their own wonderful suggestions. Be prepared to listen to your youngsters and to adjust your vision based on what they are itching to write. On the other hand, this unit will work best if children work not alone in a genre, but with other kids, and it will be tricky to oversee too many writing clubs, so do keep an eye on how many different genres kids sign up for, and plan to limit it to a manageable number.

Then too, teaching children to develop ideas that matter to them and to write (perhaps in new formats) about things that they understand and have experienced is a critical part of this unit. Every decision that a writer makes ultimately depends upon her relationship to the idea about which she is writing. You will therefore want to help children select topics that inspire them but also that they know something about based on either firsthand experience or research. The child wanting to write about hiking Mt. Everest might instead write about biking up a steep hill or might be channeled to engage in research. That is, you may need to rein in—or redirect—children's imaginations just a little.

Help students get started with their writing by reminding them of the steps in the writing process. Writers will need to make decisions around topic and genre, as well as what kind of paper best suits their choices.

After rallying children around this idea of self-selected writing, remind them of what they already know how to do. This might sound something like, "Writers, you already know so much about writing. You know how to come up with ideas for your writing and choose paper. You know how to plan, and you know that you don't have to wait until you get close to publishing to start the important work of revising. And you know how to make writing easy to read by editing for spelling and end punctuation. You will use all of this to make all your own decisions—from topic choice to paper choice. You will decide how your writing will look, what your writing will sound like, and where in the library your writing will go." Keep in mind that this unit is all about the writing process and helping children move through the process with independence and resolve. You will want to bring out or create a chart of the writing process and put it in a central location. You could even create individual process charts to go into student folders, and to show children how they can keep track of their movement through each step of the process. Your process chart might look like this.

How to Write Anything:

1. Think of an idea.

2. Get paper.

3. Touch each page and say what will go there.

4. Sketch the pictures.

5. Write the words.

6. Reread to see if you can make it even better. Make changes if you need to.

7. Put it in the "done" side of the folder and start all over again.

Be sure to add easy-to-understand picture clues for each step of the process so your students can read and understand the chart independently.

In a way, it will be as if you start the unit by making a small keynote address to your writers. On the same day, you will want to launch your children into the actual work of independent writing. This means that you will teach them how to generate a topic, choose or create their own paper, plan out how their story or poem or how-to or letter will go, and get started writing. You might want to say, "Ask yourself, 'What do I want my writing to look like? Do I want it to be a poem? A song? A picture book? A book that teaches all about a topic I know well?' Turn and tell your partner what you have in mind for your writing project."

One of the ultimate goals that you have for all of your students is for them to become self-directed, deliberate, and confident writers who are deeply engaged because they have taken ownership of their writing. This unit, with its focus on student-selected genres, supports this kind of autonomy.

Students' first step will be to choose (or design) the kind of paper that makes sense for the writing projects they each have in mind. If you have writers who have decided to write picture books, you might suggest they use the same paper they used during the *Writing for Readers* unit or "Storytelling across the Pages." Children who want to create a how-to might use the same paper they used in the *How-To Books* unit, while children who want to write a letter or make a card for somebody might take a blank piece of paper and either write their letter or fold it in half and make a card from scratch. By this point in the year, you know your children well, and you can stock your writing center with the kinds of paper that will match the particular interests of your students. Will your students jump at the chance to write fantasy or superhero stories? Maybe you'll leave a stack of paper with a border of stars and rainbows for writing magical stories. Did your students love making observations during the "Looking Closely" unit? Perhaps you'll stock the writing center with a basket containing zip-top baggies filled with objects from nature for students to use as inspiration for their writing. This might be a time to include some fancy materials from art so that kids have access to different colors and media if they choose to make cards or pamphlets.

Remind your kids that although all writers always take time to plan for writing, some projects require a little bit more time to develop for planning than others.

BEND II: LIFTING THE QUALITY OF WRITING

Reinforce the habits, processes, and qualities of good writing.

You may find that children are so excited about choosing their genre that their volume goes up drastically, but that meanwhile there is, at first, a dip in the quality. You need not worry. As Carl Anderson wrote in *Assessing Writers* (2005), when children "lose control" of their writing, it is often a sign that they are trying out more sophisticated techniques. This is where your teaching becomes the lifeline of this unit. Clearly, since all children will be working in a different genre, the work of this unit becomes teaching—and often-times, reinforcing—the habits, processes, and qualities of good writing that your students work on each and every day in writing workshop.

Then, too, you'll want to remind children that the characteristics of good writing are fairly stable across genres. Whether a child is writing directions or songs, it is equally important to write with precise, exact words, to reread to make sure the meaning is clear, and to answer readers' questions as one writes. You might pull out old charts and exemplar texts to remind children of some of the strategies they already know for making their writing come to life: make sure their pictures really show the action in the text, that the people aren't just floating in the air; make sure that everything in the picture is also in the words; tell a story (or directions) bit by bit, step by step so that the person reading it can imagine the story and act out all the steps.

Utilize writing partnerships and publishing houses as a means for writers to both give and receive feedback.

Your students will have ample opportunities to practice responding to feedback from peers and adding details to strengthen their writing as needed, in keeping with the end-of-the-year expectation most state standards hold for kindergartners. You will want to remind children of all they know about what makes a good partnership, ways partners help each other during different stages of the writing process, and how partners encourage each other to stay focused on goals. Project partners might decide when and where to meet, as well as how often.

At this point in the year, you will expect children to be adept at talking about their pieces with one another and giving each other compliments and feedback—with some support and guidance from you. Remind them to be specific—pointing to and naming a particular strategy the writer used well and proposing a next step. As you assess the partner work that will be critical to their projects, teach them how to read each other's writing as readers.

Now is the time to put to use the publishing houses that you created in Bend I. Children can meet in their writing clubs to offer one another support and feedback. If your class won't be confused by some cross-club interaction, you could mix things up a little by suggesting that children writing in different genres compare similar crafting techniques that they have effectively used. Writers could gather together, Post-its in hand, read their pieces, and provide feedback to one another.

Foster revision by making sure that all prior charts and revision tools are made available to students. Encourage students to take their topics and revise across genres as well.

You'll want to coach children to use the revision strategy charts in your classroom, which you have likely been referring to all year, as well as the Information, Opinion, and Narrative Writing checklists, to help each other revise their writing. Teach them to ask questions as they sit side by side, using the charts as a reference. For instance, one partner might say, "You used speech bubbles to show what people said. Are there any other places where you could try the same thing?" Also, when it comes to improving the quality of writing, you will probably remind your kindergartners to get out their revision tools. Flaps and strips, thin markers, Post-its, extra pages, carets, and asterisks are all signals that your kids are going back into their writing to try to make it better. In this unit, you will find it especially helpful to lean on these very concrete symbols of revision to help make sure your children are working on quality, as well as quantity, in their writing.

One surefire way to ignite new energy for revision is to let children know that writers sometimes revise by looking at their material and thinking, "What else could I make of this?" Just as Degas revised his drawings of ballet dancers to be etchings, pastels, paintings, and sculptures, kids can take that favorite story about making pizza with *Abuela* and revise it to become a poem to *Abuela*, or a "how-to make pizza" book.

One of the great joys of this unit will be the fact that children will emerge as different writers because no two writers will be working on the same exact thing. Even children who are working in the same genre will tend to produce their own versions of that kind of writing, especially with some encouragement from you. Now is a time to take risks. Perhaps one child will write a funny rhyming poem, while another child will write a more serious prose-like poem. You might even encourage your strong writers to create projects that blend genres: a how-to pamphlet that tells kids how to do something good for the environment, like recycle or compost; a mystery that begins with a cryptic chant or song. Encourage your children to explore and have fun.

You will definitely want to capitalize on children's emerging writing identities. If one child writes a gigantic book of jokes and another writes a how-to-tap-dance book, let each child become famous for what he or she has done, developing an identity as a particular and unique kind of writer. You may want to develop a chart that celebrates every child's expertise. Children can add to this themselves, coming up with interesting ways of describing the work they've mastered.

BEND III: USING MENTOR TEXTS AS OUR PERSONAL WRITING TEACHERS

Support students in using mentor texts independently through full-class minilessons and small-group work in writing clubs.

By this time in the year, your children will have had several experiences using mentor texts. Your work with mentor texts in this unit, however, will be a bit different, because students are studying a variety of genres. While you can teach full-class minilessons walking students through the steps of selecting mentor texts, much of your work with them will likely take place in small-group settings.

As children begin this work, teach them that when using mentor texts to find ideas for their writing, they need to first notice a part they like. Once they have that part, they then need to try to name the specific craft move the writer used and figure out how the writer did it. Finally, your writers can try this same craft move in their own writing by selecting a part in their work where it would be beneficial to incorporate that same move. Students need not wait for you to teach them all about different genres then. If they know which genre they want to try out (a poem, for example), make these mentors available and allow writers to examine them as they write.

You can meet with students in their writing clubs to support them as they undertake this work. As students meet with their peers, they can talk about mentor texts, maybe using little Post-its to mark the pages or whole texts that they want to try out and then sharing with their group what they chose and why. Don't let your students' mentor text selections be restricted by their independent reading level. If you need to read the book to the students in the group and walk through the process of noticing craft moves step by step, all together, so be it. The important work here is that students are learning from the authors that they admire.

You might say, "Writers, you already know how writing teachers live all around us. I am one of your writing teachers, your partner is one of your writing teachers, your writing club is a whole community of teachers, and the authors that we've been studying all year are your writing teachers, too. In this new bend of our genre study unit, you will continue that relationship. Choose any author that inspires you to write this new kind of book. If you are the kind of writer who wants to write a superhero story about Spider Man or the Hulk, or maybe you want to write a fairy tale or a song or a poem, or maybe you want to write talking-animal stories like Mo Willems's *Piggy and Elephant* books, whatever kind of book or piece of writing it is that you want to write, find a writer who writes just like you do! Writers, the possibilities, like your ideas for books and stories, are endless."

Nudge your students toward independence; highlight students in the class who can serve as genre experts.

At this point, you will gear your teaching toward the habits, processes, and qualities of good writing that independent writers possess. Now, more than ever, is the time for you to teach your students to mine their repertoires, understand the power of each genre to communicate a message, find authors that inspire them, and put those pieces together to create the kinds of writing projects that inspire others.

Some children will choose genres you have not taught previously, and you'll find it helpful to gather these students together and teach them a few key strategies for writing in that genre. You may also enlist the help of kids who have been particularly successful with a genre: "If you need help with your poem, you might want to ask Chastity." Now is a good time to gather tips for writing in particular genres onto charts. For instance, if a few kids want to write greeting cards, your tips might be something like, decide what kind of card you want to make (what occasion, for whom), create a message that matches the purpose of the card, and make sure your message is for the person who will get the card. As children do their own writing and study mentors in one genre or another, encourage them to add to the list of tips you've begun for them.

BEND IV: PREPARING FOR PUBLICATION

Teach students to make independent revision decisions. Remind them of revision strategies and tools that they have used throughout the year.

As the unit winds down, children will choose one of their projects to publish. In units past, you might have said to your students, "Today, when you revise, you might want to add speech bubbles to remind yourself where in your story someone talks," and then, predictably, all of your children may have added speech bubbles. Since this unit is about true independence, we suggest that, instead of teaching kids which way you want them to revise their pieces, you teach them to think about what their pieces need to be the best they can be. Refer them to your shared classroom charts such as "When We Are Done, We've Just Begun" or one on elaboration, and direct them again to the Information, Opinion, and Narrative Writing checklists.

Remind children that revision strategies include cutting, stapling, adding into the middle of a page, and resequencing. Of course, you want them to know not only the physical work of revision but also the reasons for altering a draft. Remind them that writers put their work into the world for other people to read, and so we want to make sure that it's clear to readers, that it says what we want it to say, and that it jumps off the page for readers, making them laugh, smile, nod in agreement, or sigh.

Teach revision strategies that work across genres: adding more to pictures and words, showing and not telling, adding details, revising beginnings and endings, rereading, and considering audience.

Certainly, you will want to nudge children to add more to both their pictures and their words. A child who has written about jumping waves with her dad might notice that she can say more about how the sun sparkled on the water or about seagulls flying overhead in a *V* formation. In addition, children can add actions. They can think about exactly what their bodies were doing (in stories) or what they imagine them doing (in poems)—maybe their arms are flapping or their feet are tapping or they are curled up in a ball—and what the people or animals are doing too. For example, in *Sheila Rae's Peppermint Stick* by Kevin Henkes, Sheila Rae stumbled, the books fell, the stool tipped, and the peppermint stick broke. We really can picture what happened here. This is a nice place to remind children of the envisioning work they do in reading. They picture what is happening when they read, so they need to create a picture for their reader when they write. This is the building block for showing not telling, through actions.

Adding details is an important part of revision too. Remind children how to reread their pieces thinking about which part is the most important. Often, this will be the very thing that made them want to write their piece in the first place. If kids are having a hard time figuring out the most important part, they might ask themselves, "Where in my story do I have the biggest feelings?" This is the part we want children to stretch out with details that spotlight what makes this moment essential. For example, a child rereading a story he wrote about cooking *arroz con pollo* with *Abuelo* on Saturday might realize that the most important part happened when he and his *abuelo* smelled something burning. This might be the part of the story he will want to develop further, adding in dialogue and small actions.

You may also want to remind children that they can add new beginnings or endings. Show them that they can try writing a few different beginnings or endings and then think about which one works best. One way to have kids try out new beginnings and endings is to study some mentor texts. Being able to name what the writer did in his or her beginning or ending can be a useful step for young writers who are working on their own beginnings and endings.

Above all, encourage children to reread. They will have already learned the importance of this, and now you will have the opportunity to spotlight it again. Remind children to reread not only entire pieces but short sections too, asking themselves if what they've written is clear, if a reader would understand it, if they've written exactly what they intended to say. Tell children to notice both how the writing sounds and how it looks. Are there spaces between words? Punctuation? Do the words look right? Children can work in partnerships, showing each other places they've revised and helping each other plan possible revision strategies. They can act out stories and how-tos together to make sure they can picture what is happening and to find places to add more actions or talking or feeling or thinking. Children can read and reread their stories to their partners, using the Narrative Writing Checklist and together thinking more deeply about their pieces.

You might also encourage children to picture their reader reading their piece when it is all finished. Do they envision the reader laughing? Feeling scared? Likely, children will find places they need to revise to achieve that effect. Again, children might want to draw on the mentor text they have been using to see how that writer makes the piece scary or funny, for example, and use what they notice to add to their own writing. They could also read their pieces aloud to partners to see what kind of reactions they get.

Teach students that writing needs to be readable.

Children will then edit their pieces with input from a partner and guidance from you. You'll want to remind them that whenever they write for readers, they need to make sure they write with punctuation, spell words as correctly as they can, and reread their writing often, making sure it looks right, makes sense, and sounds right. This is also a good time to make sure that kids are using any editing checklists they have developed together in other units.

FANCY UP THE WRITING AND CELEBRATE!

When it comes time to make finishing touches, children can think about all the ways they have polished their writing so far this year and decide which ways will work best for these new projects. Do they want to add dedications and "about the author" pages? Do they want to create blurbs on the back of the books? Do they want to use different materials from the art center to make the covers of their books? Mentor texts will also serve as a great source of inspiration.

As the unit winds down, you'll want to make choices about the kind of class celebration you and your children will hold. The kinds of texts they create will certainly play a role in this decision, and a museum of writing is often a great way to display a variety of writing genres. In this instance, children will display drafts, mentor texts, and published pieces for visitors. As these visitors tour the museum, children can discuss the reasons for their choices in both genre and publication. After the museum, once the guests have bid farewell, children might take a quiet moment to reflect on what they learned about themselves as writers in this unit and make goals for themselves for over the summer. Or, after visiting a neighborhood bookstore, the children might set up the classroom to resemble a bookstore with separate sections for each genre, posters advertising "Meet the Author" events, and an area for author readings. You can record these readings and put them up on a class website. Some schools have scanned the children's books and then displayed them on a virtual bookshelf.

In addition to whatever end-of-unit celebration you and your class dream up, you may want to leave some time for children to look back at all of the writing they have accomplished over the course of the school year. Independently or with a partner, they could look at their published pieces and reflect on all the different kinds of writing they have done this year and on how much they have grown as writers. You could even set aside a day for students to read aloud their favorite piece, to a partner or to the whole class. You may decide to keep their writing energy going by talking to them about the kinds of writing they will be doing in the next unit or even the next year. This is a time for both reflection and celebration of all that they have done and all the ways they have grown as writers!

Part Two: Differentiating Instruction for Individuals and Small Groups:
If . . . Then . . . Conferring Scenarios

THERE IS NO GREATER CHALLENGE, WHEN TEACHING WRITING, than to learn to confer well. And conferring well is a big deal. It matters. If you can pull your chair alongside a child, study what he or she has been doing, listen to the child's own plans, and then figure out a way to spur that youngster on to greater heights, that ability means that you will always be able to generate minilessons, mid-workshop teaching points, and share sessions that have real-world traction because these are really conferences-made-large. However, knowing conferring matters doesn't make it easier to master. Even if you know that learning to confer well is important, even if you devote yourself to reading about the art of conferring, you are apt to feel ill-prepared for the challenges that you encounter.

I remember one child who was trying to reread his writing. The boy looked at the page, then squinted up into the sky. His teacher, at the boy's elbow, coached, "Usually it helps to look at the word." I thought to myself, wise move. But the little boy continued to look upwards. After half a minute, he said, "Sometimes God tells me the word." What does a teacher say in response to that?

Or what do you say to Matthew who brings you his story, and you read it and you think, "I don't know if I could write it that well?" Still you talk, Matthew responds, and you leave the interaction with the terrifying realization, "He's doing everything! I don't know what to teach him."

Then there's Alexandra. You confer with her on Monday, and again on Tuesday, and again on Wednesday, using every scaffold and every trick in the book, and absolutely nothing seems to stick. It's as if she is made of Teflon.

If you have had conferences like these and end up wondering what's wrong, know that you aren't alone. Teachers across the world find that conferring well is a challenge. Most of us have, at one time or another, written questions on our hands, or on cue cards, that we want to remember to ask. Many of us have mantras that we repeat to ourselves, over and over. "Teach the writer, not the writing." "It's a good conference if the writer leaves, wanting to write." "Your job is to let this child teach you how to help."

Many of the books on conferring will help you understand the architecture of a conference. You'll learn to research first, then to compliment, then to give critical feedback and/or to teach. You'll learn tips about each part of a conference. When researching, follow more than one line of inquiry. If you ask "What are you working on?" and hear about the child's work with one part of the writing, don't jump to teaching that part of the writing until you generate a second line of inquiry—whether it's "What do you plan to do next?" or "How do you feel about this piece?" or "If you were going to revise this, what might you do?" There are similar tips that you'll learn about other aspects of conferring too.

But you will no doubt feel as if there is another kind of help that you need. You will probably want help knowing not only *how* to confer, but also knowing *what* to teach.

Visiting hundreds of schools has given me a unique perspective on that question, a perspective that may be difficult to come by when you are in one classroom, with one set of children with very particular needs. After working in so many schools, with so many youngsters, I've begun to see patterns. I notice that when X is taught, children often need Y or Z. I meet one Matthew in Chicago and another in Tulsa, Oklahoma. I meet Alexandras in Seattle and Shanghai. And I've begun to realize that, despite the uniqueness of each child, there are familiar ways they struggle and predictable ways in which a teacher can help with those struggles. Those ways of helping come from using all we know about learning progressions, writing craft, language development, and grade-specific standards to anticipate and plan for the individualized instruction that students are apt to need.

The charts that follow are designed to help you feel less empty-handed when you confer. I've anticipated some of the most common struggles you will see as you teach narrative, opinion, and information writing through the units of study in this series and I've named a bit about those struggles in the "If . . ." column of the charts. When you identify a child (or a group of children) who resembles the "If . . ." that I describe, then see if perhaps the strategy I suggest might help. That strategy is described in the column titled "After acknowledging what the child is doing well, you might say . . ." Of course, you will want to use your own language. What I've presented is just one way your teaching might go!

Often you will want to leave the writer with a tangible artifact of your work together. This will ensure that he or she remembers the strategy you've worked on and next time you meet with the child, it will allow you to look back and see what you taught the last time you worked together. It will be important for you to follow up on whatever the work is that you and the youngster decide upon together. Plan to check back in, asking a quick "How has the work we talked about been going for you? Can you show me where you've tried it?"

Some teachers choose to print the "Leave the writer with . . ." column onto reams of stickers or label paper (so they can be easily placed in students' folders). You also might choose to print them out on plain paper and tape them onto the writer's desk as a reminder.

 I hope these charts will help you to anticipate, spot, and teach into the challenges your writers face during the independent work portion of your writing workshop. (The charts are also available in the online resources.)

Narrative Writing

If . . .	After acknowledging what the child is doing well, you might say . . .	Leave the writer with . . .
Structure/Cohesion		
The writer is new to this particular genre. When you ask the writer to read you the story, she tells/reads the names of the things on the page, speaking in a way that doesn't sound story like. "This is me. This is my dog." Even if the writer has said more, the text seems more like an information text or a catalog of items or attributes than a story. "I like the beach. The beach is hot. I have fun at the beach. It has sand."	You have told the reader all about (your topic) and that is what writers do when they write an all-about book. But you are writing a story. When you write a story, it is important to tell the reader about the things that happened, telling what happened first, and then next, next. One way you can do this is to touch the things in your picture and tell what you did, or tell what happened. Then your reader can know what is happening.	A Post-it that has a picture of a person doing an action. Then you might leave the writer with the words, "What happened?" or "Who did what?" Who did what?
The story is confusing or seems to be missing important information. The writer has written a story that leaves the reader lost, unable to picture what is happening or to understand the sequence of events. Either he left out important actions, or he left out significant people that he meant to include in his story.	You know what? I'm confused when I read this! I'm sort of going, "What?" "Huh?" And I really want to understand what exactly happened. The way writers tell stories that readers can understand is they remember what happened first, and then after that. They put what happened into the picture and write it in their stories. Sometimes, though, do you know what happens? Writers FORGET to put down some really important information that readers need to know. It helps to reread your writing and find places where you can say more to help your readers get a clearer picture of what happened. After you write a story, reread it and ask yourself, "Is this confusing? Can I give the reader more information to make this part clearer?" (Sometimes reading your writing to a partner can help you find the places that might be confusing to a reader.)	I reread. When I go: Huh? (??) I add (^) to make it clear. Reread: 1. Did I tell what happened first, next? 2. Can I say more? 3. Can I answer readers' questions?

If . . .	After acknowledging what the child is doing well, you might say . . .	Leave the writer with . . .
There are multiple stories in the booklet. On each page of a story booklet, the writer has written about a whole different event. For example, she may have herself at the circus on page 1, swimming in a pool on page 2, and going to school on page 3. There is no sense that this is one unfolding story.	You know what you have done? Instead of writing one WHOLE story, bit by bit, in a book, you have used this book to list the different stories you could write. OOPS. There is actually special paper for making a list—(see, you could make a shopping list on this paper, or you could list story ideas on it.) But what we are doing now in our writing workshop is we are taking booklets and writing one whole story in each booklet. Let's try this first idea from your list—a story about swimming in the pool. What did you do right before you got in the pool? That goes here, on page one. Then what did you do next? . . . Touch this next page, say what happened. Then turn to the next page and think, "What happened next?" That's it! That's how writers write stories.	A Post-it that is divided into two columns, with list paper on the left, and a story booklet on the right. The first page of the story booklet shows a character doing something. Plan: 1. Think (a drawing of a person, thinking of someone doing something) 2. Touch and tell 3. Draw each page 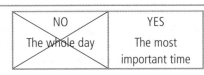
The story lacks focus. This writer has told a story that spans a great deal of time and therefore has no detail. The story may tell about the whole trip or the whole summer. This could also be a bed to bed story, which may start "I woke up" and end, "I went to bed" or may start, "We packed our lunch," include climbing the mountain, and end, "We came home." For kindergartners, you won't be apt to worry if the event spans a few hours—driving to the beach, being at the beach, playing in the waves, coming home—but if it is so unfocused that there are no details, you'll want to teach the writer to focus "on one thing you did."	You told me a little bit about a lot of things that happened to you. What famous writers usually do, like the writers who write the books in our library, is they decide which one is the most important thing they did, and then they write the whole story of that one thing, writing with a lot of details. Right now, will you look through the pages of your book and think, "What's the one part of this that is the story I really want to tell?" You might want to rip off the pages that are about things that aren't that important. THIS is the important part, right! Now you know what famous writers do. They take the one most important thing, and they write a WHOLE BOOK just on that one thing. So (grabbing a blank book), what is the first thing that happened when you did . . . Oh! Whoa! How did that go? Who said what? Okay, so it starts . . . Then what? Can I stop you? You're on your way, writing a whole book about just the most important part of your story. After this, will you always remember that you aren't writing about the whole day, you are writing about one thing you did or one thing that happened?	

If . . .	After acknowledging what the child is doing well, you might say . . .	Leave the writer with . . .
Elaboration		
The writer has created a story that is sparse in pictures and words. This writer's work is sparse, given what the writer can do. It may be that the writer has just drawn a few icon-like pictures on the page, with no detail or elaboration in the drawing. It may be that the writer has written something, but the writing is sparse, like a single sentence that summarizes the whole page. "My mom and I went to school." If there is writing, it is about the main character and the main event, only.	When I read your story, it is hard for me to picture the whole thing, because you didn't tell me that much detail about what is going on, about all the people, and the place, and the things that are happening. You just put this little bit of stuff on the paper. You have to tell more so I can picture the story! One thing that you can do as a writer is that after you are done (and I push back in my chair and shake my hand out, as in a "Whew! That's done" move) you can pull back in and look at your pictures and your words and think, "What else can I add?" Think: who? And really imagine who was there with you. Think: what: and really imagine what you were doing Think: where? And add in some details about the place. Draw it and then write more and more and more!	Who? Where? What? (Remind the writer to use details in his pictures and words.) You might leave a copy of a page of your writing that has details in the picture and in the words. On top of the writing you can write, with bold marker pen, "Who?" "Where?" and "What?" Arrows from those words can point to details about the people, the place, the activity. Alternatively, you can leave a note: When you are done, you've just begun. Who? ☺ Where? 🌳 What? 🏃
The writer spends more time adding insignificant details to the picture, rather than elaborating with words onto the story. This writer spends her time during writing workshop drawing rather than writing. She doesn't use her drawing as a form of rehearsal to generate more writing, so much as an alternate activity. She spends her time adding in small details such as eyelashes, seven cars on the road, and all the people in the baseball stand.	I want to suggest that you are ready to start spending MUCH more time writing, so you write about this much on each page, and write about five pages in a day. That'll be very grown up. To do that, you are going to need to do your drawings differently. Instead of trying to tell everything in pictures, you are going to need to tell a lot more things in words. What I do is I sketch the main thing that is happening on a page, and then after I have drawn just the main thing, I pause and think, "Do I know what I could say?" And if I can think of the words to say, I start writing. And I push myself to write and write and write, telling the whole story in words. Sometimes after I have written a lot and I feel like my hand is tired from writing, I go back to the picture and I add more stuff into it—but you know what? That gives me ideas for MORE that I can write, so then I go back to the writing. I look at what I put into the sketch and make sure everything that I've drawn goes into words, too. After you finish your book, you can come back and look at your picture and make sure that everything you have drawn is in your words, too.	A Post-it that contains an icon that shows a piece of paper with a smallish picture space and a larger writing space, with a sample picture and words. The arrow can point to the words. There can be dotted line arrows, off the sides, going from from the picture to the words in a fashion that suggests that content that is first in the picture later gets added into the words. 

If . . .	After acknowledging what the child is doing well, you might say . . .	Leave the writer with . . .
The writer tells action, action, action, and seems to not elaborate on any of the options. This writer does not yet use or have a repertoire of ways to elaborate on a moment. This writer's story only has actions. "I went to the park. I went up the slide. I went down the slide."	You write like this: (I stand up) "I went to the park." (I take one step) "Then I went down the slide." (I take another step) "Then I went on my bike." (I take another step). Your goal needs to be to tell more with each step. Here, walk with me. (Now, walking in stride) "I went to the park." (In a whisper) Say more. Which park? How did you get there? Let's try it again. (Walking together) "I went to the park." Child: The one down the street. We drove there. "I went down the slide." (I gesture to add on) Child: I went fast.	A Post-it saying: One step (say more!) The next step (say more) The next step (say more) Alternatively One step (which one? How? Why?) Next step (which one? How? Why?) Next step . . . .
The writer overuses one kind of detail more than others to elaborate. This writer will have one kind of detail that she overuses in her story. For example, she may write a personal narrative that uses, almost exclusively, dialogue throughout the piece.	You have a lot of talking in your story! In fact, it is so much talking it is TOO much. It sort of goes like this "Hello. Hello. How are you? I am fine. I am going to the store. Okay I am too. Bye. Bye." I can *hear* what people are saying but I can't *see* what people are doing. When you write a story, try to remember to tell who is doing what, where. Then you can add a little bit of talk, but just a little bit.	A picture of speech bubbles attached to drawings of stick figure people in action, in a place. The caption: Who, is doing what, where? A little bit of talk. Who, is doing what, where? A little bit of talk.
Language		
The writer has few if any words on the page. This writer has used pictures to depict the story, and there are few if any labels, and no sentences.	Who's this? It's you!! I didn't know. You have to tell us. Write "me." You can write that—just say it slowly, mmmmmm/eeeeee. Say it. That's it. What is the first sound you hear? Write the letter for that sound. Great. Read that. Do you hear any other sounds? So now you have written "me." What is this? I didn't know! What do you have to do? You are right. You need to write the word. And you know how, don't you? Say it slowly . . . So . . . when I come back, there should be about 6 words on this page, because after this, you need to remember that writers don't just draw pictures, writers also write. It is really important that you label *everything* that is on the page. Keep going until all the pictures on the page have a label or two, then move on to the next page!	A drawing of the child's page, with 4–5 labeled items on it.

If . . .	After acknowledging what the child is doing well, you might say . . .	Leave the writer with . . .
The writer has words on the page, but they are difficult to read. This writer has written with strings of letters. She has left few spaces, if any, between her words. This writer may only have one or two sounds that are accurate in her words, which makes it difficult to read her sentences or labels.	After you write, go back and reread. Right now, will you reread what you have written on this page? (The writer gets stuck.) Let me try. (I work at it, and get stuck.) Let's try writing another word, and I'll show you how to write it so you can read it. Which thing do you want to label? Okay, this. Get started, and let me watch. (The child starts, and hears and records the first sound only. She is done.) What I'm noticing is that you say the word, hear the first sound, and write that down. But then, you are done! If you want to write so people can read it, you need to say the word again and hear more sounds. Try it. That's it. So after this, when you go to write a word, try to say it one time, record what you hear. Then reread what you have written and say it again. If you get a lot of sounds down, when you come to the place where there are no more sounds, leave a little white space. That will show people you are done.	Not: . . . . But: I g t s . . . . I go to scl.
The Process of Generating Ideas		
The writer struggles with thinking about an idea for a story. This writer often sits for long periods of time contemplating what to write. He tends not to have many pieces. This may be because he does not use a strategy to help himself, or it may be that he does not think the things in his life are worth writing about, or he may have distractions that prevent him from self-initiating.	One thing that you can do as a writer is make a list of possible ideas for stories. You can use our chart, ways to come up with ideas for stories, to help you think of all the many things you have in your life to write about! Then you can pick one and write it. When you are done, you come back to the list and pick another!	Story Ideas 1. _____ 2. _____ 3. _____ 4. _____ 5. _____

If . . .	After acknowledging what the child is doing well, you might say . . .	Leave the writer with . . .
The writer returns to the same story repeatedly. This writer has many pieces about the same event. For example, the writer may have three stories, all about biking in the park.	It is nice to write a couple of stories about the same thing—like Cynthia Rylant has a couple of stories about Henry and Mudge, right? And you have a couple of stories about the park. So you are sort of like Cynthia Rylant. But one thing about Cynthia Rylant is she doesn't have Mudge get lost in this story AND in this one AND in this one. He gets lost in one story, he is in a dog show in another story, and he gets in trouble in another story. After this, if one story tells about you bike riding in the park, what could the next story tell about? What else do you do in the park? Great. So, you and Cynthia Rylant are going to be a lot alike, because each of your books will tell about something different.	Stories in the Park 1. bike riding 2. finding a baby bird 3. ??  To come up with a story idea, think of: • Things I like to do • Places I go • People I enjoy spending time with 
The Process of Drafting		
The writer starts many new pieces but just gives up on them halfway through. When you tour the writer's folder, you see many pieces that are unfinished. This may be because the writer abandons the piece to start a new one or it may be because the writer does not get a chance to finish the piece on day one, and on day two the writer does not look back in her folder to decide what to work on. Rather, she starts a new piece each day.	Each day in the workshop you have a decision to make: to work on a piece on the green dot side, pieces that are not finished yet, or start a new piece. When I look at your folder, I see you have many pieces that are on the green dot side that are not finished! That's so sad . . . all those unfinished stories. How awful. Don't you think those stories deserve to be finished? After this, why don't you look through the green dot side of your folder and see if there is a story that isn't finished. That story is probably calling to you, saying "Finish me!!" So—hear the stories call, okay, and reread it. Then think, "What happens next? What else was happening in this story? How does it end?" When you have written the ending, you can reread and revise it like always. Then you can put it on the red dot side.	A "Reread me first!" sign on the green dot side of the folder. Ask : What happens next? How does this story end?

If . . .	After acknowledging what the child is doing well, you might say . . .	Leave the writer with . . .
The writer tends to write short pieces with few words or sentences. This writer may have several pieces in her folder, but she has few words or sentences written in each story. It seems as though the writer may not spend a great deal of time on a piece. She may write a couple of pieces in one sitting. This writer tends not to reread her pieces or try to push herself to say and write more on the page.	What I am noticing about your stories is that they tend to look like this (I make a quick page with a sparse drawing and a single squiggle for a line of print). But I think you, as a writer, are ready to make stories more like this (and I make a quick page with a much more full drawing, and 5 lines of squiggles, representing print). What do you need to go from this (I point to the first drawing) to this (I point to the second drawing)? Right now, will you try a new story and make it more like this? (the second way). Show me how you get ready to write. Okay, will you do that again, but this time when you touch and tell the story on each page, will you touch the top of the writing and say what you will write first and then touch the middle of the writing and say what you will write next and then touch the bottom of the writing—on that page—and say what you will write last. Like this: I put the worm on the hook. (I touched the top of the page.) Now, instead of jumping to the next page—where I catch a fish, I'll say more. I got worm gook on my fingers. (I touch the middle of the page.) It was disgusting, the worm kept wiggling. (I touch the bottom of the page.) Now I can go to the next page.	A Post-it with "Write long and strong." or "More, more, more!" written on it. (As you leave the Post-it, remind the student to use the classroom chart to help her remember ways to add more to her writing.) 
The writer's folder lacks volume of pieces. This writer tends to have very few pieces in his folder, maybe one or two. He tends to go back to the same piece each day and add more. Usually the additions are sparse, maybe a word or two. Perhaps the writer is spending more time adding to the drawing.	Last night at home, I was looking for your work . . . and I looked (I imitated looking and finding little) and I looked (I looked under the folder, around it) and I looked!! And I hardly found any work. What do you think has gotten in the way of you getting a lot of work done? Child: I get stuck a lot. Well, after this, when you get stuck, you are going to have to get help so you get unstuck—and fast! Because you need to get a LOT of writing done. Let's make a plan. Today, I am pretty sure you can fill these pages of your book, so I am going to write "Monday" on these pages. Tomorrow, what do you think you can get done if you don't let yourself get stuck? So let's label those pages "Tuesday." Now . . . you have a lot to do. So will you remember, touch the pages and say aloud what you are going to write, then come back and write it. And if you get stuck, ask for help. Come get me. Because you HAVE to meet these deadlines.	Have I added all that I can? 1. Reread and ask yourself, "Did I add all I can add?" 2. Check with a tool: an exemplar, book, or chart. 3. Add more if you can. 4. When you have tried all you can, start a new piece. 

The Process of Revision

If . . .	After acknowledging what the child is doing well, you might say . . .	Leave the writer with . . .
The writer rarely adds to the writing without prompting and support. When asked, "How do you know that you are done?" the writer tends to say she is done because she is on the last page. She tends not to reread her writing to consider adding more or revising. When prompted or reminded to reread and think about what she can add, the writer is willing to think and add more to her writing.	One thing writers do, when they finish their last page, as they reread the whole book and think, "What else can I say? What else happened in this story?" They turn back to page 1 and use their pictures to help them imagine more and use the movie in their mind to capture more details on the page.	Revise: Make a movie in your mind. (Leave an icon on the Post-it with a movie camera.) Make a movie in your head.
The writer usually adds to his writing rather than taking things away. This writer tends to elaborate on each page of his writing, usually adding in more details about what he did and said and how he felt. He rarely takes out parts or information that do not belong, relate, or make sense to the story.	When writers revise, they don't only add more to help show what is happening and how they feel. They *also* take things out that don't belong or make sense in their story. One thing you can do as a writer is to revise and take things out that don't belong. One way to do this is to reread and ask yourself, "Does this belong in my story? Does it make sense?"	Revise: 1. Does it belong in my story? 2. If no, X it out. 1. Does it belong in my story? 2. If no, **X** it out. Revise: • + add information • − take out information
The writer tends to revise by elaborating, rather than narrowing and finding the focus of the piece. This writer tends to revise only by elaborating on the story. She does not think about revising the structure or focus of her piece. She is not the type of writer who tears off pages to find the important part of her story to say more about it. She tends to add more to each part, regardless of the focus.	Writers revise by adding more. They also revise by thinking about showing the important part of their story. They think, "What do I really want to show and tell my reader?" And they revise accordingly. One thing that you can do before you try to add on to your pieces is ask yourself, "What is the most important part of my story?" One thing writers do is take off the pages that aren't about that part and add more pages to tell about that important part. They try to add their details about the important part of the story.	Is my small moment about the important part? Or does it have unimportant parts to take out? <table><tr><td>Important Parts</td><td>Not Important Parts</td></tr><tr><td></td><td></td></tr></table>

If . . .	After acknowledging what the child is doing well, you might say . . .	Leave the writer with . . .
The Process of Editing		
The writer does not use what he knows to edit his piece. When this writer is rereading his work, he edits very few things. When you prompt the writer or remind him to edit and fix up his writing, he is able to do so.	One thing that writers do when they have revised their stories as best they can is that they reread their pieces and edit their mistakes. They fix their spelling and their punctuation the best they can. One way to do this is to reread your story carefully, from start to finish, a couple of times. You might first reread it to make sure that there aren't any missing words and fix up any easy errors that stand out, like ending punctuation you missed or spelling that you wrote too quickly.	Reread and Edit • Find missing words • Fix spelling • Check punctuation
The writer does not know what in her piece needs editing. The writer, while editing, may skip over many words and miss many opportunities to fix punctuation. She is unable to find many of the errors she has made. She is not always sure what she is looking for and therefore may be overwhelmed.	Sometimes when you are editing, there may be times when you feel like you can't find any errors! That's when you really have to challenge yourself. One thing that you might do as a writer is to choose a couple of words to think more about—ones that you aren't sure if they are spelled correctly. You can choose them and think, "Are there other ways to spell this word? How else could it look? Is there another way to make some of these sounds?" You might try the word a few different ways to see if you can find a better spelling.	Try Your Spelling a Few Times: 1. _____ 2. _____ 3. _____

Information Writing

If . . .	After acknowledging what the child is doing well, you might say . . .	Leave the writer with . . .
Structure and Cohesion		
The writer is new to this particular genre. This writer may actually write in another genre. Instead of writing an information book about her topic ("All about Dogs"), she may end up writing a narrative about her topic ("One day I took my dog for a walk.")	You've got a nice start to a story here. You are telling one thing that happened—you took your dog for a walk. But actually, right now we are writing all-about pieces. The pieces we are writing now aren't stories, they are all-about nonfiction books that teach people true stuff about a topic. One thing that you want to do as a writer is to teach your reader the information about the topic, rather than tell them a story about one time when something happened to you. To do this, one thing you might do is name the topic and the information that you can teach your reader. Say the list across your fingers, and then you can draw and write it across pages.	Teaching Book: • Name a topic • Teach information (You may leave the writer a couple of nonfiction books from the leveled library to help her remember what an information book is.) *Teaching Book:* *Name a topic.* *Teach information*
The writer has included facts as he thinks about them. This writer tends to write without planning. He starts writing any information that comes to mind and in any order. The result is a text with information that is not grouped together on a page or in a chapter.	You know what I think is happening? You have so much to say that when you pick up your pen, you just start writing right away, without thinking, "Wait. How will my book go?" I'm glad you have a lot to teach, but now that you are getting to be almost six years old, I think you are old enough to do what professional writers do—the people who write the books in our library. When they sit down to write a book, instead of just starting by writing one thing that comes to mind, they say, "Wait a minute. How will my whole book go?" and then they plan out what they will write about on one page, and on another page. Are you willing to try that planning while I am here to help? Yes?! Great. And after this, whenever you go to write a book, remember to do like the pros and to say, "Wait. How will my whole book go?" Then you can plan by making a table of contents, or by sketching what goes on each page.	WAIT! How will my whole book go? 1. Table of contents 2. Pictures *WAIT! How will my whole book go?* *1. Table of contents* *2. pictures*

If . . .	After acknowledging what the child is doing well, you might say . . .	Leave the writer with . . .
Elaboration		
The writer provides information in vague or broad ways. This writer's books are list-like, with broad terms and few supporting details. "Dogs play. Dogs eat. Dogs sleep."	When you are teaching information, it is important to teach your reader lots of information—on every page, you teach the reader some information. One way that writers think up details to teach is by thinking, "What would readers want to know about my topic? What questions would they ask?" Then writers answer those questions.	Page 1: Information Page 2: Information Page 3: Information **Ask and Answer Questions** • Why? • When? • How?
The writer writes with lots of good information but it is in helter-skelter order. This writer may have written about two, three, or even four different topics in one book. Or, he may not know how to organize his information.	You know what, your writing hops back and forth from one topic to another to the first again . . . like it is about bears, then dogs, then bears again, then dogs, then rabbits, then bears . . . it is sort of *crazy*! Usually what a writer does is she puts all the pages that are about one thing together, with a title, and all the pages about something different together, with a title. Maybe you want to use jaws (the staple remover) to take your book apart and see if it can get divided into three books. And another time, when you are writing a book and you think of a whole different topic to write about—get another book. Don't smush it all together in one.	(One topic) (one topic) (one topic)
The writer invents or makes up information about the topic in order to elaborate. This writer may invent facts. Usually this information is made-up. It is not rooted in personal experience or any sort of research from books or photographs or other artifacts.	When writers write fiction stories, they make up stuff that isn't true. But you are writing NON-fiction now, or true books. After you write a book, you can reread it and think, "Is this all true?" And if some of it isn't true, then you take it out.	Reread: • True information? Or • NOT true?

If . . .	After acknowledging what the child is doing well, you might say . . .	Leave the writer with . . .
Language		
The writer does not use all that she knows about letter sounds/vowel patterns to write words. When you read the writer's work you see that she has one or two letter sounds in her labels. You know from your letter name/sound ID assessment that she knows the other letters and sounds that she is not putting onto the page. When you read the writer's work you see that she has a few words misspelled with vowel work that she is working on in word study. From your spelling assessment, for example, you know the writer knows or is working on short vowel patterns. In her work, though, she does not write with short vowel patterns.	When you write, you want to use all that you know about writing words. Using *all* that you know will help you as well as your reader to read back what you have written and taught in your book. One way that you can help make your writing even more readable is to work on getting more sounds in your words. After you put a letter down for your word, keep saying the word slowly. Listen for the next sound. Slide your finger under the letter you wrote as you listen to the next sound. Keep your alphabet chart here to think about what other letters you hear.	You may decide to have your student use her word sorts to help her study her spelling. Remind the writer to take out her sorts to remind her about the features of phonics that she is studying and working on. These could be in an envelope that she keeps in her writing folder if you make her a set.
The writer does not use domain-specific vocabulary. This writer has not included specialized words that fit with his topic. For example, if he is writing about dogs, he might say, "This is a dog. You need to walk your dog. Dogs need food. Dogs have babies." The writer does not specify what kind of a dog (a Spaniel or a Maltese), the type of food that dogs eat, or what you call baby dogs—puppies.	When you are teaching information in your books, remember that the reader *also* wants to be an expert. Usually experts know really important words that have to do with their topics. As a nonfiction writer you want to use these words and also teach them to your readers, so that they too can be experts. As you are writing, one way that you can do this is to reread and think about the information and ask yourself, "Did I use all the special words that fit with this information? Is there a better word or a more specific word that fits with this topic that I can use?"	A Post-it with a few keywords to reread and think about. You may write on the Post-it, "Look for places to use special words. Think about what important words fit with this topic." special words
The Process of Generating Ideas		
The writer chooses ideas that she likes rather than what she actually knows information about. This writer tends to pick topics that she does not know a lot of information about. Sometimes she picks topics according to things that she likes or once saw on a television program. The writer does not pick topics with which she has had personal experience.	Sometimes it seems like you are trying to write Information Books about topics that you don't know too much about. That doesn't work. Writers write books about things that they know and care A LOT about so that they can teach others. They usually choose topics that they have *a lot* to say about and that they think is important for others to know. There are many ways to come up with a topic to write about. You can think about your own life. What are things you have, places you go, or things you do that you think other people should care about as well? Let's make a little list. Then you can start thinking about the chapters or parts of your book to see if you have a lot to say about the topic.	To come up with an idea for an information book, think: • Things I have • Places I go • Things I like to do Information Book Things I have. Places I like to go. Things I like to do.

If . . .	After acknowledging what the child is doing well, you might say . . .	Leave the writer with . . .
The Process of Drafting		
The writer spends more time elaborating on his drawing than using the picture to help add and write more information. This writer often does not spend the workshop time in an efficient way to get as much information and words as possible down on the page. He spends most of the workshop time drawing details onto the page, rather than using his drawing to get more words on the page.	Writers draw and write with details to teach the reader. Sometimes you may spend more time on your drawing because you see a lot of details that you can add. Remember, while writers are drafting, they are trying to get as much information into their words as possible. Drawings can help the writer see more to say. I want to teach you that when you are drafting and revising your information books, use what you draw to help add more information to your words. If the details don't really help you add more information, wait until the end of the writing process when you will publish to color and illustrate.	Use your picture to write all that you see.
The Process of Revision		
The writer is unsure how to revise her writing and does not use the various tools in the classroom. When this writer gets to the last page in her book, she may stop and get another booklet to begin a new text. The writer does not go back and try to add to her piece. She may or may not be aware of the charts, checklists, and mentor texts that she could use to help her decide how to revise her text.	Information writers revise as well. They use the same types of tools as other writers to help them revise their piece. Sometimes, studying a mentor text can help you find and think about what you may want to add or change in your own writing. One thing that I want to teach you is that you can study books and think, "What did this author do that was powerful in his writing? Can I do the same thing with my topic?"	A mentor text to help remind her to study books to find ideas for her writing. On a Post-it, write, "What did this author do that I can do?"
The writer tends to revise by elaborating, rather than narrowing and finding the focus of the text or chapter. When this writer revises, he may always revise to add information to his piece. Rarely will he think to take out something that doesn't go or to improve the way he has said something.	You are really good at adding things as you revise. Sometimes you add details, and sometimes you add things that will help make it so your writing makes sense. That's great. Congratulations. Now—can I teach you the next step? The next step as a reviser is to reread your writing, knowing that sometimes what the writing needs is for you to add, and sometimes the writing needs you to subtract! Like, if the book is called My Hamster and you get to a part that goes on and on about your turtle . . . what would you need to do? You are right! Subtract. And what if you say "My hamster has a tiny tail" at the start of your book and then at the very end you say, "My hamster has a tiny tail." What if you repeated yourself by mistake? You are right! You'd subtract. Writers even do one more thing when they revise, they sometimes try to write the same thing with better words, or more excitement—revising not to add or subtract but to improve. If you ever do that, would you call me over?	**Writers revise by:** • + adding (details, answers to readers questions) • – subtracting (parts that don't belong, repetition . . .) • improving (making the words better, making writing interesting)

The Process of Editing

| The writer edits quickly and feels done, missing many errors.

This writer tends to miss many errors because he does not reread his writing. | When you reread and edit your writing, it should take a little bit of time. You shouldn't feel like it was super fast. Editors are detectives, looking for mistakes that are hiding!

One way to edit really carefully, like a detective, is to reread your writing *many* times, out loud, and slowly. Place your pen right under the words as you are reading. You might even reread a page a couple of times, just to be sure that no mistakes are hiding. Use the checklist in our room to help remind you of what kinds of things to be looking for as you are rereading. | Reread and Edit:

• Spelling
• Punctuation
• Capitals

Reread and Edit
the dog rn — Spelling!
Capitals! Puncuation!
✓ The dog ran. |

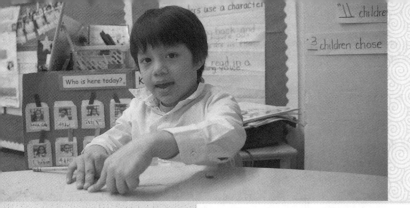

Opinion Writing

If . . .	After acknowledging what the child is doing well, you might say . . .	Leave the writer with . . .
Structure and Cohesion		
The writer is new to the writing workshop or this particular genre of writing. This writer may be writing a story or an informational text and may not understand how or why to write opinions.	You are writing a story—it tells what happened to you first, next, next. You want to be the kind of writer who can write different kinds of things. Like if you were a jewelry shop, you'd be glad if you could make pretty pins, but you'd also want to know how to make other things, too. And you wouldn't want to start off making a necklace and it looks like a little dog with a pin on the back! Well, today, you sort of did that. You started out making not a necklace, but some opinion writing to change the world and you ended up making . . . a story again. When you write opinion pieces instead of telling a story, you tell people how you feel about things in the world—things you really like or things you want to change. Then you say, "This is what I think, and this is why."	Story: I did this, and then this (or she did this, then this.) Opinion writing: I think this. Here's why! You should think this way too. *Story	Opinion* *I did this, then this, then this.* *I think this because . . .*
Elaboration		
The writer is struggling to elaborate. This writer tends to not have much on the page. The writer may be able to tell her opinion and give some related information about the topic.	Writers try to give their readers lots of information about their topic and their opinion so that readers begin to believe and understand the writer's feelings about the topic. One way you can add more is to ask and answer the question, "Why?" "Why do I have this opinion? Why is this important?" This can help you say more. You can also tell an example, or tell what is bad about the other side of your opinion.	Say more: Why do I feel this way? Why else? What's bad about the other side?

If . . .	After acknowledging what the child is doing well, you might say . . .	Leave the writer with . . .
The writer uses some elaboration strategies some of the time. This writer may elaborate on one page in his writing. But the writer does not continue to elaborate and use what he knows in other parts of his book.	One thing that you can do as a writer is to study your own best writing—and then try to do that best writing on every page. I say this because on this page, you used a very fancy technique to elaborate . . . let me show you. . . . So what do you think you should be doing on this page? And this one?	Study great writers: like YOU!!! What did I do on one page (in one part) that I can do on every page (in every part)? Page 1: Page 2: Page 3: I compared two things!!!! Page 4:
The writer's piece lacks voice. This writer's piece sounds very formulaic. She doesn't yet really talk to the reader.	Right now, will you tell me a bit about this? What do you think? Oh . . . and can you explain why you think that? You know what—one of the most important things that writers learn is that great writing sounds a lot like the writer is talking to the reader. Let me say back what you just said to me because these words are full of what people call voice. These are the words you should put onto the page when you write. Listen . . . I'm telling you this because the way you wrote this book, and this one too, and this one, it feels like a machine could have written that. It doesn't *sound* like you. Would you work on making your writing sound more like you? The best way to do that is to do what you just did—say aloud what you want to write, and say it like you are talking to another person. Then put those words onto the paper.	At the top of each page, draw a face with a speech balloon coming out of the mouth to remind the writer to first say it to someone, trying to talk like she really cares about it. Remind the writer that you'll check to see if it actually sounds like the writer (not a machine) wrote it when you read her writing.

If . . .	After acknowledging what the child is doing well, you might say . . .	Leave the writer with . . .

Language

| **The writer struggles to write longer or "harder" words on the page.**

When the writer encounters something new or something that he needs to approximate, he freezes up. This writer might not feel comfortable writing words he doesn't already know. For instance, the writer may be stymied by writing the word *delicious*. The writer may stop writing or may write the word *good* instead. | Sometimes it seems to me that you are about to write really long and hard words, and then you start thinking, "Oh no, maybe I won't spell them right. Oh no, maybe I'll make a mistake, Oh no, Oh no." (I've meanwhile been shaking in my boots.) When you feel like you might chicken out because you are worried about making a mistake—say to yourself, "Stop it! Be Brave!" And then, even though you aren't sure, just try the best you can and keep going. That's the way to get the best writing onto the page.

If you chicken out from writing big words, or from writing the little details that can help a reader, or from trying to say something in a really beautiful way, your writing ends up just being so-so. The only way to make great writing is to be a brave writer.

And to be a brave writer of long and hard words, you can think about each part of the word and think if you know other words that sound the same as that one.

You can even try the same word a couple of times. Then you can pick the one that sounds the best and looks right. | Be BRAVE!

Think about the parts of the word as you spell.

    pumpkin

    pump/kin

Be BRAVE!
pumpkin
pump kin |
| **The writer tends not to use specific and precise language as she writes about her opinions.**

This writer writes with generalizations. ("We need stuff because it is good. It is nice. It is great.") | I want to tell you something about your writing. You tend to write with big general words, and it is usually better to write with exact words. Like instead of saying, "Our coat closet is bad," it would be better to say it with exact words. "Our coat closet is . . . what?" Messy? A snarl of coats? It looks like people just throw things anywhere? You see how it is better to use exact words than big general words like, "It is bad."

Try asking yourself, "What *exactly* do I want to say?" Think about one way to say it, then think about another way. | What EXACTLY do I want to say?

Think about one way . . . then think about another way!

What exactly do I want to say?
1   2 |

The Process of Generating Ideas

| **The writer is stymied to come up with an idea for writing.**

This writer often sits in the workshop wondering what to write about. He does not believe the things that he knows are worth writing about. He does not yet use a repertoire of strategies to find ideas that matter to him. | Writers can find ideas all around them.

In fact, one thing that you can do as a writer, right now, is look around this classroom. What things do you see, what problems are there, or what things could you make better?

Looking around you, whether you are in school, at home, or in the community, you can always find things to write about. | You may help the writer generate a list. Write these ideas down on a Post-it. |

If . . .	After acknowledging what the child is doing well, you might say . . .	Leave the writer with . . .
The writer writes one piece, then, another, without making any one her best.	You are writing a lot of fast pieces. Yesterday you wrote three pieces in one day. Congratulations. Are you ready for the next challenge? Because once you can do that—once you can come up with an idea and write it quickly—the next challenge is to come up with an idea, and *not* write about it. Instead, you think of another, another, and you list them across your fingers. *Then* you choose the very best idea, and work on that piece of writing for a really long time to make it the longest and the best piece you ever wrote. Are you willing to try that? So first: list possible ideas. Then: choose one. Then: write the best piece you ever wrote in your whole life.	**First:** list possible ideas. **Then:** choose one. **Then:** write the best piece you ever wrote in your whole life.

The Process of Drafting

The writer doesn't have a plan before he begins to write. This writer seems to pick up his or her pen, and write what he or she wants, and then is stymied. The writer might then start an ending to the piece, only to decide more needs to be said. This can lead to a piece that is chaotic, or that has a sequence of four endings.	One thing I notice about you is that when you write, you sit down at your desk, pick up your pen, and you get started. Lots of kids wait and wait and wait to think up an idea, but you don't wait. Ideas come to you right away, and that is great. But I want to teach you that when an idea comes to you, it is good to *not* get started writing but to instead spend some time getting ready. The way writers get ready is they plan what they are going to say so that before they write a word, they have a whole lot of ideas for what will go at the beginning of the piece, and in the middle . . . I think it would help you plan your opinion pieces if you did some drawings before you start writing—planning drawings. Maybe you could try starting with a drawing of the problem, then one or two drawings of what you think people could do, step one and step two, to fix the problem, and then a drawing of what things will be like when they are fixed up. So today you are writing about the park being messy—what will go in the first drawing, the drawing about the problem? Okay—so beautiful birds and flowers and then garbage. Will you put some details in—like show a daffodil with a paper cup smushed right on it? Great! Then that drawing will help you plan out about six things you can say about the problem!	A Post-it that helps remind him how to get words down on the page. You may write, "Use your plan." There may be an icon of a page of writing with picture space and writing space. There should be an arrow pointing to the picture space for the writer to use to help add to his words. Planning paper—two pages taped together, divided into four columns that are labeled: Problem Fixing it, step 1 Fixing it, step 2 The solution

If . . .	After acknowledging what the child is doing well, you might say . . .	Leave the writer with . . .
The Process of Revision		
The writer fills the pages as she drafts and only writes to the bottom of the page when she revises. This writer tends to push herself while she drafts to write to the end of the page. The writer, therefore, sometimes feels like she cannot or does not need to revise because there is not enough space.	It seems like you get to the end of the page, when you are writing, and you stop there. But lots of times, I am pretty sure you have more to say—but you aren't going to page two, or adding on a flap at the ending. After this, will you remember that writers write as much as they have to say . . . and they make their books longer, their pages longer, so they can say everything? They ask themselves, "Do I have more to say?" And if have more to say, they *find* the space. They *make* the space. Whenever you want to add more, you can think, "Should I add a flap or a whole new page?" And then just tape or staple it in!	Extra flaps and strips to use and add onto her page. To help the writer to remember to use these tools again the next day, you may tuck a few into her writing folder. This way, as she is trying to add more, she will have a few flaps ready to add on. You may leave a Post-it that reminds her to add on to her writing. It may say, "Revise" at the top, and underneath it may say, "Add on information, examples, and reasons."
The writer tends to have a limited repertoire of how to elaborate on his topic. This writer elaborates by adding on to his piece with the same strategy, rather than using a few ways to say and add more.	I notice that you elaborate by (strategy the writer is using) in your opinion books, and that is great. BUT writers try to write with a variety of stuff. So I wanted to remind you that opinion writers also say more by adding in these things: Tips on how to do something Suggestions on the best ways to do something Warnings about what could go wrong Stories of other people who have done this Encouragement to do this Let's reread your piece and think about which ones we can add.	If you made a whole-class chart on ways to elaborate in opinion writing, you could make a mini version of that chart for the child's writing folder, or you could turn that chart into a checklist.
The Process of Editing		
The writer edits for one thing but not for others. This writer may edit her work but only tries to fix her spelling. She may not reread to fix her punctuation.	When writers edit, there are many things that they look for and try to fix. You can use a checklist to help you think about editing for many things. You may want to reread your piece a few times, looking for different things each time.	Reread and Edit! • Spelling • Punctuation • Capitals
The writer only uses or knows one way to edit his spelling. This writer may feel like he has edited his spelling, even if few words are actually fixed. This may be because he does not have or use a repertoire of ways to work on spelling. For example, he may only check his piece for word wall words. He may not try out multisyllabic words in different ways to help get a closer approximation or the correct spelling.	Young writers use more than one strategy to spell. As you are spelling a word, you can try to think about what is the best way to spell this word—the word wall, trying to write and rewrite the word a few times, or looking it up in a resource in the room.	Try Different Spellings: 1. _____ 2. _____ 3. _____